Sidney

THE LAWYER'S UNCOMMON GUIDE TO
COMMERCIAL LEASING

SECTION OF REAL PROPERTY | TRUST & ESTATE LAW

ABA

Defending Liberty
Pursuing Justice

Cover design by Mary Anne Kulchawik/ABA Publishing.

Library of Congress Cataloging-in-Publication Data

Saltz, Sidney G., author.
  The lawyer's uncommon guide to commercial leasing / by Sidney G. Saltz; Section of Real Property, Trust & Estate, American Bar Association.
     pages cm
  Includes bibliographical references and index.
  ISBN 978-1-62722-609-7 (alk. paper)
  1. Commercial leases--United States. I. American Bar Association. Section of Real Property, Trust, and Estate Law, sponsoring body. II. Title.
  KF593.C6S2584 2014
  346.7304'3462--dc23
                          2014021585

Contents

Preface

Being a commercial leasing lawyer involves a lot more than knowing what forms to use and how to use them, how to draft or review leases, or even how to negotiate them. There are so many leasing situations and so many important lease provisions that familiarity with them is really essential if one is to be an effective counselor and advocate for one's client. The purpose of this book is to provide some of that familiarity.

I would like to start by giving some information about myself and about my experience. I am a general commercial real estate lawyer, practicing in the field for over 40 years. I have handled all kinds of transactions, including purchases and sales, financing, project development, and leasing. Leasing is a special love of mine as I have represented landlords or tenants in connection with industrial/warehouse leases, office, retail, and ground leases. I have been active for many years in the Real Property, Trust, and Estate Section of the American Bar Association, chairing committees in the Leasing Group and also serving a two-year term as chair of that Leasing Group. I have also written extensively about leases in various journals and lectured, with my friend and client, Steven Podolsky, an experienced real estate broker, on the subject at many programs, including, for over 20 years, programs for brokers offered by the Society of Industrial and Office Realtors (SIOR). I invite you to find out more about me and my practice by seeking out my website, http://www.sgsaltz.com.

In 2010, the American Bar Association published the second edition of my book, *From Handshake to Closing—The Role of the Commercial Real Estate Lawyer*. It is a primer, principally for young lawyers, and to assist in the training of law students about the practice of real estate law.

The American Bar Association is currently publishing my new book, entitled *The Broker's Practical Guide to Commercial Leases*. It contains much of the material Steve Podolsky and I taught in the SIOR courses, plus a lot of additional information intended to assist brokers in their representation of landlords or tenants in commercial leasing. In the process of reviewing and editing that book, it became obvious to me that it contained much of the knowledge about leases and leasing that I have learned over the many years I have been representing landlords or tenants as an attorney, in every type of lease that could be thought of, and that much of that knowledge could also be of use to leasing lawyers, to prospective leasing lawyers, and to law students considering a career in real estate law. For that reason, I have prepared this companion book, incorporating most of the text of the *Broker's Guide* into this, a general guide to commercial leasing for lawyers and law students.

Except in the case of the discussion of letters of intent (which are very important in leasing), I have not duplicated the material in *From Handshake to Closing—The Role of the Commercial Real Estate Lawyer*. Each book stands on its own.

In doing a lease transaction, the lawyer must consider many issues other than the contents of the leasing document. Many of those issues will be discussed in this book. I will start by describing various property types and leasing situations; they will inevitably have vital effects on the lease agreements relating to them. Then I will address various lease provisions that are usually found in all leases, whether they are industrial/warehouse, office, retail, or other. I will also consider how leases within each category may differ, based on the physical situation and the nature of the deal. Finally, I will discuss provisions unique to leases pertaining to each of those types or uses. I hope the reader will not only find this book interesting, but that it will assist him or her in the practice of the rewarding field of commercial leasing.

In both *From Handshake to Closing—The Role of the Commercial Real Estate Lawyer* and *The Broker's Practical Guide to Commercial Leases*, I dealt with the relationship of lawyers and brokers. That relationship is often more adversarial than it need or should be. While I will not duplicate what is said about that in the *Handshake* book, I would like to point out that the role of each professional is to represent the client and to get the best fair deal for that client as can possibly be obtained. In the event of a disagreement, the decisions must ultimately be made by the client, whose satisfaction with the total product of the professionals' work is their joint objective. This companion book thus presents a common ground for brokers and lawyers, a place where each can receive information useful in their work that is common to both of them.

I have mentioned my lecturing for SIOR with Steve Podolsky. Much of the *Broker's* book, and this book, as well, is based on those lectures and also on input by Steve in his review of my manuscript for that book. I have dedicated that book to Steve and, in all fairness, I am pleased to do the same in connection with this one. I very much appreciate all I have learned from him, and thank him for that, as well as for our many years of working together, traveling together, and simply being good friends.

Letters of Intent

1

A letter of intent may be used to encapsulate the terms of the lease in an abbreviated manner. It is generally used to establish the key terms of a deal before the formal agreement is prepared and executed. Unfortunately, letters of intent are very often signed without attorney input.

If the lawyer is consulted, the first question to be considered in evaluating a letter of intent is "When are letters of intent binding?" This leads to the next question, that is, "For what purpose?" Are they binding for the purpose of creating an obligation to negotiate in good faith? Or are they binding as an agreement between the parties as to the terms and conditions of the transaction?

I do not propose to discuss the many cases on letters of intent that deal with those issues—for that, I recommend to you an excellent article by Thomas C. Homburger and James R. Schuller entitled "Letters of Intent—A Trap for the Unwary[1]". In that article, the authors determine that, depending on the jurisdiction, the answer may turn in part on the language in the letter of intent and in part on other evidence of the intent of the parties. In other words, even though there may be language in a letter of intent stating that it is not intended to bind the parties to an agreement until a final agreement is written up, executed, and delivered, the parties may in fact be bound. At the very least, a letter of intent

---

1. 37 Real Property, Probate & Trust J. 3, 509 (Fall 2002).

may create an obligation to negotiate in good faith, unless that is expressly negated in the document.

Brokers like letters of intent. First, but not necessarily foremost, the letter of intent may result in the entitlement to a commission, based on the broker having found a "ready, willing, and able" tenant or purchaser for his or her client's space. More often, however, commissions are not really earned until a lease is signed, so we should not impute negative motives to brokers. No, brokers like letters of intent because they document the basic terms of the deal and facilitate the drafting of the lease or contract document.

Usually, letters of intent drafted by brokers contain language that negates the intent to create a binding agreement, but as noted above, it may not be entirely effective. Often, a broker representing a tenant will make a "request for proposal" (an RFP) to the landlord or its broker and receive a detailed response that will contain the business terms of the deal. Sometimes, the broker representing the tenant or buyer will make an "offer" setting forth the terms on which the tenant is willing to enter into the lease or the buyer is willing to enter into a contract. That offer may be "accepted" or may be subject to a "counteroffer." I put the words in quotation marks because the offers, acceptances, and counteroffers are not really intended to be used in the context of creating a binding agreement, and they probably do not do so for several reasons. First, it is understood in the trade that it is not their purpose. More importantly, the broker does not usually have the authority to bind his client to a lease or contract. The actual parties do not customarily sign the papers being exchanged (unless, of course, there are no brokers involved). The problem really arises when the brokers take the terms that have been discussed, either orally, by RFP, or by offer and acceptance, and reduce them to writing in a letter of intent and ask the parties to sign them. Remember that, at this point in time, it is most likely that neither party has consulted its attorney.

Let us assume that I am consulted at that point in the process. Whether I represent the landlord or the tenant, my advice is, "Don't sign!" By signing, the parties may create a binding agreement, even though important matters have not been dealt with, or have been dealt with in an imprecise manner.

Even if the letter of intent is accurate and contains all sorts of language about not creating a binding lease, there may still be problems. The problems may be made worse by making the letter of intent very detailed. I have seen letters of intent that were extremely long and contained almost all of the terms of the agreement, using, in many instances, the very language contained in the lease proposed to be entered into. I do not believe that any amount of language that states that the letter of intent is not binding (except, perhaps, conditions such as approval by the party's governing group, such as a board of directors of a corporation or members of a limited liability company) could keep that letter of intent from actually being enforced as the agreement between the parties.

What are some of the other problems with letters of intent?

While a major purpose of a letter of intent is to discourage each party from seeking a better deal before the current negotiations are wrapped up, some letters of intent actually require the landlord to cease marketing the property during negotiations. In representing a landlord, I strongly object to that provision (if I see it in advance) because it places what I deem to be intolerable burdens on that party. That party may have to incur the cost of removing large and expensive "For Rent" signs (and replacing them if the deal does not go through), but that is a minor matter compared to the requirement that the client turn away prospects when it does not have a firm deal. The problem is more serious when the tenant is to be afforded a period of time to conduct its due diligence or obtain zoning or permits, at the end of which period it may terminate the proposed deal, leaving the landlord with no alternative tenants.

In addition, the letter of intent may create an obligation to negotiate in good faith, and the refusal to agree to some important term may result in a claim (and litigation) that the party has failed to live up to that obligation. That puts particular pressure on the parties subsequently negotiating the lease, especially if, in the course of negotiation, issues are raised (and agreed to) that are inconsistent with the terms of the letter of intent. I experienced an example of this some years ago. A landlord client signed a letter of intent that committed the landlord to forego certain additional rent pass-throughs.[2] The tenant asked for a larger build-out allowance

---

2. "Pass-throughs" is shorthand for additional rent based on taxes and various operating expenses incurred by the landlord in connection with the property. They will be discussed at length below.

than was contemplated by the landlord (the issue was not clear in the letter of intent). The landlord granted the concession, but changed the lease to restore the pass-throughs and sent a red-lined copy of the lease to the tenant, highlighting the change in the pass-through language. The tenant signed the actual red-lined copy of the lease (implying that it had reviewed the changes since the prior draft), but then sued the landlord, claiming that the lease did not accurately reflect the agreement of the parties. To avoid protracted litigation and expense, the landlord settled the case.

Under the circumstances, what do I recommend?

1. The parties should not sign letters of intent. I mean that in two senses. The parties should avoid using letters of intent. They will, however, probably use them because they have some advantages. In that case, they should not sign them or give a written authorization to any third party to sign on their behalf; if they do, they may be deemed to have complied with the Statute of Frauds and be bound by the terms of the letter of intent without meaning to be.[3]

    There are alternatives to letters of intent that are far less dangerous. For example, I recommend using a term sheet. It states, in essence, that "the following are the terms on which the parties propose to lease (or sell or purchase) such and such property" and then only the basic terms are set out. It is always wise to provide that it is not a binding agreement and to set out a date after which either party may terminate discussions without liability. It may even expressly negate an obligation to negotiate in good faith. Vagueness is the key. If the parties do not sign the letter of intent and the Statute of Frauds applies, the letter of intent does not bind the parties. There are two caveats. First, if a broker signs for a party, it should be clear that he is without written authority to bind the party. Second, beware of the Federal Electronic Signatures Act. A letter of intent sent via e-mail by a person who is

---

3. Most jurisdictions have enacted the "Statute of Frauds," which provides that contracts for the sale of real estate and leases for a term in excess of one year must be signed by the party to be bound. In Illinois, the applicable provision of the Statute of Frauds is codified in 740 ILCS 80/2.

employed by one of the parties and who has authority to sign a lease may satisfy the requirements of that Act and bind the party.

2. If parties must use and sign a letter of intent, it should contain language negating the intent to create a binding agreement. If possible, conditions to the conclusion of a lease should be inserted. Examples of those conditions are board approval. tenant's confirmation of the zoning or condition of the premises, in its discretion, or the landlord's satisfaction, again in its discretion, with the tenant's financial condition or its operation of its prior premises.[4] If the obligation to negotiate in good faith is not negated, time periods should be provided for the delivery of the draft lease or contract and for the completion of the negotiations, after which time the parties will have no obligations under the letter of intent.

3. If you represent the landlord, recommend to your client that it not agree to take the space off the market.

Unfortunately, it is unlikely that the lawyer will be consulted before a letter of intent is signed. To ensure that he or she has a chance to review it, the lawyer must know that the deal is contemplated, that a broker has been hired, and that a deal is imminent. It will take a very close relationship with the client or the broker for the lawyer to have that kind of information.

---

4. It is my feeling that the word *discretion* really means discretion, and that commonly used phrases such as "sole discretion", "absolute discretion," and "sole, unfettered, and absolute discretion" are not necessary to get the concept across.

Types of Premises 2

People who deal in or have an interest in real estate tend to think in terms of three types of premises: industrial/warehouse, office, and retail. Many would also add, among the basic types, vacant land and land with a building to be demolished.[1] Actually, the selection of types of premises is much more diverse and complicated.

In the industrial/warehouse scenario, the premises may be an entire building or in a multi-tenant building. They may be in (or on, as in the case of a telecommunications lease) a single building or in part of an industrial park (now customarily called by fancier names, such as "business complex"). They might even be part of a larger complex of commercial uses, including office, retail, or even some residential. They may be located near an airport, or in an area that had (or continues to have) heavy industrial uses, or in an area that was previously totally undeveloped.

The office situation may be even more diverse. The premises may be in a single-tenant, single-story building; a multi-tenant, single-story building; a single-tenant multi-story building; a multi-tenant, multi-story building; or a multi-use building, with retail on the lower floors. Some buildings even have residences on the upper floors. The building might have general use office space

---

1. Agricultural and mineral leases, although important, are not within the scope of this book.

only, or it may include or be exclusively for medical use. It may be located in the central business district, suburbia, or even exurbia.

Retail is also very diverse. The space to be leased may be located in a regional mall, a community shopping center, a strip center, or a multi-use building (including office and/or residential). It may be freestanding. It may be a multi-story department store, a big box, or a supermarket—every shape or size, down to the mom and pop neighborhood food store or barber shop. It may be located in a central business district, in an upscale retail street, in a suburb, on a commercial street, or even in a residential neighborhood.

Vacant land, or land that is under a building to be demolished, may be located anywhere and be of any size.

Of course you know all of this. You see it all around you. I just discuss this to highlight what follows next—the discussion of different uses and different lease situations.

Different Uses and Different Lease Situations 3

Industrial/Warehouse Leases—Uses

The uses to which this type of property may be put are as varied as American industry and commerce. They may include heavy manufacturing, although I suspect that most companies that operate that type of plant own their own facilities. Most industrial/warehouse leases that involve manufacturing will be for light manufacturing or assembly. Still, those uses can present substantial problems for owners. For example, the use or repackaging of chemicals may create environmental problems or be corrosive to the space and the roof (depending on how the fumes are ventilated), or to the heating, ventilating, and air-conditioning systems. A food processing facility may create odor or vermin issues or use a lot of water, which can affect the finished surface of the floor.

I recall a situation where a seafood processor in a multi-tenant building promised the landlord that his operation was clean and did not create uncontrolled odors, and in fact the landlord checked out the processor's prior facility before leasing to it. However, the tenant's assertion turned out to be untrue, and the adjoining tenants complained bitterly about the smell. Fortunately, the lease prohibited odor problems and the landlord could evict the tenant. Unfortunately, the odor had entered into the cinder block demising walls and continued to be a problem for an extended period of time.

Heavy equipment may damage the floor. The bearing capacity of the floor will have to be determined before leasing to a user that has heavy equipment. The user may have to dig a pit in the floor to operate equipment. Provision will have to be made in the lease for the restoration of the floor to its original condition. A use may require a great deal of electricity and conduit or bus duct running in places that may be inconvenient for a subsequent user, or that may be useful to the next user, but as to which there may be an issue of ownership.

I worked on a lease where the tenant was a bread bakery. Its operation required very prompt delivery of its products to maintain freshness. That was to be accomplished by having trucks drive into the premises on one side, be loaded, and then drive out the other side. The tenant required street-level truck entry and exit and truck doors at either end of the premises. Needless to say, not many users need a configuration like that, so the landlord required a large security deposit to pay for the restoration of the opposite wall. The tenant argued that it should not be required to pay for restoration at the end of the lease because the landlord might find another user who would require in and out truck doors. Although that was like the needle in the haystack, the landlord in that case agreed to market the premises for such a use before the expiration of the lease and for a short time afterward, but if it was not successful, or if it leased the premises for another use, the security deposit was to be applied for its intended purpose.

A user might require the right to install an overhead crane. That creates a weight issue and a serious removal issue that will have to be dealt with in the negotiation and documentation of the lease.

Of course, a lot of the same issues may apply in connection with a warehouse. The stinky fish operator may have been storing the fish, not processing it, and the drive-through building may have been used by a beer distributor instead of a bakery. Also, even a light manufacturer or assembler may very likely be using a portion of its premises for warehousing its products.

An important aspect of the suitability of proposed premises may be the clear space, which is the dimension between floor and the underside of the sprinkler heads or the lights, whichever is lower. If the tenant's business is a pick-and-pack kind of operation, such as a pharmaceutical supply house (where the employees move through the warehouse and pick the items on their lists off of shelves), the merchandise must be accessible without the picker having to climb a lot of ladders. Less clear space is then desirable, since more clear space would be expensive to lease and to heat or cool, but wasted. On the other hand, massive containers of merchandise that are to be shipped in those containers need a lot of clear space. Attention must also be paid to the type of fire retardant in place in the premises. A water-based system could be a disaster for the pharmaceutical supply house or a warehouse that stores newsprint, but not a problem for a user who stores merchandise in waterproof containers.

The lawyers for both parties should become familiar with the details of the proposed use and also of the ability of the proposed premises to meet the requirements of the prospective tenant. If the parking lot cannot sustain the weight of large trucks, or the configuration of the docks does not allow semis to back into them, the proposed premises will not work for some tenants, and the lawyer for the tenant should ascertain this information as early in the process as possible. On the other hand, it may fall to the landlord's lawyer to raise the issue with his or her client if no one else does. It may also be the particular responsibility of each of the parties' lawyers (or brokers) to make certain that the zoning does not prohibit the proposed use in that location or require a variance or special use permit from the municipality, and that if there is to be construction, the physical requirements, such as those relating to set-backs and automobile and truck parking, can be met by the tenant. However, it is the lawyer's job to make certain that someone does so.

It does no good to pursue a lease for drive-through premises if the opposite wall of the premises cannot structurally support further openings, for example, or if the zoning does not permit two such driveways. If the use may create additional costs for the landlord at the end of the term, those costs should be dealt with in negotiation and documentation of the lease, and consideration should be given to securing the obligation to pay those costs. In fact, all the special use issues should be considered prior to the drafting of the lease. Once the parties are paying legal fees for lease preparation and negotiation, it is too late.

Special Issues in Industrial/Warehouse Leases

Many single-tenant industrial/warehouse leases are written on a "triple net" basis, under which the tenant pays all taxes, insurance, and maintenance. Taxes, insurance, and maintenance may be billed to and paid directly by the tenant, or they may be paid by the landlord and reimbursed by the tenant, but in either case, the tenant is paying them in full. If the building is new, "triple net" might even include such maintenance and replacement items as roof and structure (but often exclude defects in the original construction). If the building is not new, the landlord is frequently responsible for roof and structure. The lease might still be referred to as "triple net" but actually be a qualified "triple net" lease. Thus the phrase "triple net" is shorthand and a sometimes misleading way of describing the way the rent and other charges are dealt with in the lease. That is why it is important to avoid using the phrase without having the lease actually specify who pays what.

A lease in which the landlord pays taxes, insurance, and maintenance is known as a gross lease. It should be understood that the fixed rent payable under a "triple net" lease is lower than what would be charged under a gross lease or a gross lease with stops. If the landlord were asked to undertake certain costs, such as insurance, the landlord would expect the fixed rent to be increased to cover those costs and would require the tenant to accept the risk of increases of those costs. To protect the landlord's cash flow from the property, the lease may provide for the tenant to pay increases in those costs to the extent those costs exceed a specified base amount, or the amount payable in a base year. That is what I referred to above as "stops." I will discuss stops and their calculation below and also on page 131.

If the tenant is proposing to lease only a part of a building, the lease may still be written as a "net lease," with taxes, insurance, and maintenance being excluded from the fixed rent, but with the tenant being billed by the landlord for a share of those costs. That share is usually pro rata, but under some circumstances it may be calculated on a different basis. For example, if Tenant A has a use that requires a disproportionate share of the parking area, it is appropriate to allocate a larger share of the cost of snow removal and other parking lot maintenance to Tenant A; otherwise, other tenants would be obligated to subsidize Tenant A, which would be unfair and which they would not agree to. Likewise, Tenant B may have direct access to the parking area, whereas other tenants must pass through a common corridor as to which the landlord provides janitorial services. These call for allocating the cost of cleaning the common corridor to the tenants who use that service, and not to Tenant B.

The lease for that multi-tenant warehouse building might also be written as a gross lease with stops. The stops may be given as a set number, such as taxes in excess of $4 per square foot. If that is the case, the lawyer for the tenant should seek to find out the actual cost (or the actual anticipated cost) for the first year of the lease. If the actual taxes or anticipated taxes are, for example, $6 per square foot and that is the number the landlord used to calculate the base rent, the tenant is paying the extra $2 in the base rent for the first year and each year thereafter during the term as part of the excess over $4. The same issue obviously applies to the other elements of the gross rental.

Straight gross leases without stops or, as they are sometimes called, full service leases, are occasionally used. Since the landlord incurs the risk of unanticipated increases in taxes, insurance, and maintenance, the landlord will usually seek annual increases in the base rent as a hedge against that risk or may use full-service lease forms only for leases of short duration.

Another issue common to industrial/warehouse leases is the responsibility for environmental problems. Landlords will insist that tenants who use environmentally sensitive materials assume all responsibility for those materials. Tenants will want to know the existing environmental condition of the property to ensure that they will not be responsible for pre-existing conditions. Both parties may be concerned with environmental problems caused by third parties, such as the drive-by dumper or the adjoining owner. In a net lease, the landlord may seek to place that risk on the tenant, and the tenant will understandably resist that.

Finally, there is an issue that is not unique to industrial/warehouse leases—the hedge against inflation. In the 1960s, many industrial/warehouse leases for single-tenant occupancy in new buildings were written for 20-year terms (which was the term of the totally non-recourse loans used to finance the construction of those buildings). They were truly triple net leases, but they did not provide for any increases in the fixed rent over the term. Inflation simply was not a problem at that time.

It is hard to believe, but many even had options to extend at reduced rents. The theory was that once the loan was paid off and the owner did not have to service a debt, the rent was total profit, so the landlord could decrease the net rent and the tenant could benefit from the fact that there no longer was a debt to service. Those leases did not even provide for a recapture (which will be discussed on page 60), so the leases could be assigned for a fee or subleased at a higher rent, and the profit earned by the tenant.

Needless to say, landlords do not make those mistakes anymore (they make other mistakes). Landlords, instead, realize that inflation is (usually) a fact of life and seek to provide for increases in rent over the term. In industrial/warehouse leases, that is generally done by periodic increases in rent either by a specified dollar amount, a percentage increase, or an increase (but usually not a decrease) tied to the cost of living, using one of the indices published by the United States government, usually a Consumer Price Index, or CPI.[1] Those rent adjustments are sometimes referred to as "financial escalations." This, too, will be discussed further in numerous places below.

Office Leases—Uses

Most office leases are for general office use, such as corporate offices, law offices, accountants' offices, brokerage offices, bank back office space, and general business space. Offices located in the central business district may not include parking, especially in congested areas that are well served by public transportation. Offices located in suburbs or other outlying areas may well include parking. Another common office use is medical. Medical offices often have sinks in every examining room and bathrooms in the space rather than in the common corridor. Depending on the equipment used, the user may require extra floor-bearing capacity, extra power, or

---

1. For the first time in my career, we witnessed the threat of deflation during the recession of 2008. If that unfortunate condition ever occurs, I can foresee some tenants asking that the rent be tied to CPI, including reductions in CPI. It might be hard to argue against.

insulation against radiation. Sometimes offices are used for educational purposes, which means increased traffic on the elevator (often at the same time) and possibly students who are not as careful with the common areas as one would hope. A banking operation, which is somewhere between office and retail, has its own issues, since it might have a drive-through facility and special security needs. Each of these situations (and others not presented here) involves specific issues that must be dealt with in the pre-lease negotiations.

Some office buildings offer amenities that are not customarily offered in other situations. Thus, a building or group of buildings may offer a conference center, or a health club, or childcare, indoor parking, or a food venue. These amenities might be offered as a service by the building owner, or they may be areas in the building or group of buildings that are leased to operators of that type of business. Some services may be offered gratis to increase the leaseability of premises in the building (such as assigned indoor parking spaces) or may be offered on a fee basis. In either case, a strong tenant may seek to have those amenities offered for little or no extra charge.

Many office buildings are multi-use buildings. Certainly those in the central business district are likely to have retail users in the building, even if it is just a newspaper stand. Outside the central business district, it is not unusual for a bank or a restaurant to be located in the same office building. Multi-use buildings require special consideration, particularly by the lawyers representing tenants, as they create special issues for tenants. Those issues include the adequacy of parking, cleanliness, security, and, importantly, a proper allocation of the operating expenses for the building among the various users.

Existing office buildings do not customarily offer zoning issues to tenants. However, some uses may require confirmation that the zoning permits those uses. A bank with a drive-through for a teller or an ATM may suggest a check on zoning and other municipal requirements. Similarly, if a restaurant tenant in an office building wants outdoor dining, that may require special permits and will certainly require a check of local municipal regulations.

Special Issues in Office Leases

While the costs of taxes, insurance, and certain maintenance are imposed on tenants in industrial/warehouse leases, and also in retail and other types of leases, office leases in multi-tenant buildings usually seek to allocate to tenants not only those costs, but also costs unique to those office buildings, as "operating expenses." A major cost to landlords of office buildings (except in the case of single-tenant buildings, which are more like single-tenant warehouse or retail buildings) is janitorial service. That service, usually performed at night, includes cleaning of the offices and cleaning and sanitizing restrooms, emptying of trash, window washing, and the like.

Multi-tenant office buildings usually include a right of the landlord to pass the cost of operating expenses on to the tenants. Some of the leases are net leases, as in the multi-tenant warehouse building situation. Others are gross leases with stops. Sometimes taxes are included in operating expenses, but sometimes they are a separate item of cost, either net or with a stop. Insurance is usually included as well. Operating expenses will be discussed in greater detail below (on page 134).

Another major issue in most office leases is services. Whereas a warehouse may have HVAC units on the roof that provide heating and cooling to all or part of the space, the office tenant in a multi-tenant building is usually relying on the landlord's heating and cooling equipment and distribution system to keep the space comfortable. The tenant may also be relying on the building for elevators, maintenance of common areas, utilities, parking, and, as noted above, janitorial service. The lawyer for the tenant should make certain that the services the tenant expects are provided for in the lease.

If the tenant is leasing in an existing office building, the tenant will not have to be very concerned about zoning. However, if the tenant has an unusual office use, it may be wise for both parties' lawyers and brokers to make certain that there is no problem.

As in industrial/warehouse leases, landlords in office leases will be looking for financial escalations.

Retail Leases—Uses

In general, retail lease uses are to sell goods and services to the public. The user may be a general merchandise store, a grocery store, a book store, an upscale clothing store, a discount store—you know what stores sell what merchandise. However, retail uses may also include restaurants, salons, bars, banks, currency exchanges, income tax service providers, movie theaters, health clubs, schools, daycare facilities, and other such special uses. Each of those special uses represents a unique set of issues to be resolved in the lease and in the lease negotiations and may also involve zoning and regulatory issues.

Special Issues in Retail Leases

Financial escalation is a major issue in retail leases. Some leases handle financial escalation with a specified dollar amount, a percentage, or a cost of living adjustment as described below (page 116). However, in retail leasing there is an additional way (which may be used instead of the others or in addition to them). That is percentage rent.

In a lease with percentage rent, the tenant is obligated to pay a certain percentage of its gross sales, usually above a specified amount, or "break point." The break point may be an agreed sum, unrelated to fixed minimum rent, or an amount calculated by dividing the amount of fixed minimum rent by a percentage to determine the so-called "natural break point."

For an example of a natural break point, assume the fixed minimum rent is $80,000 per year, and the percentage is 6%. In that case, the break point will be calculated by dividing $80,000 by .06, the answer being $1,333,333.33. Another way of looking at this is that the rent is always 6% of gross sales, but if gross sales do not reach the natural break point, the tenant still pays a fixed minimum amount.

The lease might provide more than one break point. To do so, it would specify one break point and its related percentage, and then provide for a second or even a third break point and different percentages if gross sales exceed the amounts specified. The percentages over the additional break points may be more or less dependent on the nature of the use or simply based on the deal negotiated by the parties. Thus, the lease may provide for percentage rent equal to 5% of gross sales in excess of $1 million and up to $2 million, 4% of gross in excess of $2 million and up to $3 million, and 3% of gross sales in excess of $3 million.

There are other issues related to percentage rent. First, the lease must define "gross sales." Second, it must provide for some method for record retention by the tenant and for the landlord to have the right to audit the tenant's records to confirm that the correct amount of gross sales have been reported and the correct amount of percentage rent has been paid. Third, the landlord will generally require the tenant to agree not to compete within a specified radius of the location of the premises. Obviously, the third item is to prevent the tenant from opening a competing business nearby and diverting sales from the premises to the other location. The specified radius is usually referred to as the "trading area."[2] Percentage rent issues will be further discussed below (page 125).

It is not unusual for a tenant in a shopping center to request the exclusive right to sell its type of products on that property (and possibly other property owned by the landlord that is nearby). The obvious purpose is to prevent competition with the tenant's business. Exclusives create serious problems for landlords. First, agreeing to an exclusive might be an anti-trust violation. In addition, the requested exclusive use might be too broad. For example, a tenant that sells cosmetics might ask for an exclusive regarding the sale of cosmetics. If the landlord agrees to that broad exclusive, it has eliminated the possibility of leasing to a drugstore or a department store that sell cosmetics, but not as its primary use. The landlord may negotiate for an exclusion for those specific stores, but more likely, the landlord will limit the exclusive to the sale of cosmetics as the primary use of the other tenant. In addition, the tenant may request a provision that states that the sale of the item by another in violation of the exclusive is a default by the

---

2. Sometimes a lease might include a trading area even in the absence of percentage rent if the landlord is relying on a particular store to generate business in its shopping center.

landlord. This requires the landlord to police other tenants' operations and possibly having to terminate another lease for violation of the exclusive.

Landlords do not want to be put in the position of having to sue another tenant or being in default under the lease with the tenant having the exclusive. The way that is usually handled is to provide that the landlord "will not lease to another tenant whose primary use is [the excluded use]." If the lease contains such a provision and the landlord does not lease for that purpose but another tenant sells the prohibited goods, the landlord may require the other tenant to stop doing so as a violation of its permitted use clause, or the lease with the first tenant may permit the first tenant to sue to prevent the violation of the exclusive. Obviously, the tenant who is seeking the exclusive will want the broadest language in the exclusive in order to eliminate the competitive use and to require the landlord to be involved in enforcing it. The tenant's lawyer (and broker) should resist that.

Specialty retail leases (i.e., other than retail sale of merchandise) present other issues. A restaurant will create odors, invite vermin, have garbage storage and pick-up issues, or be open extended hours. If it is a restaurant serving food for off-premises consumption, it may create debris in a shopping center or on the adjoining street. A restaurant serving liquor or a bar will have to have a liquor license and may have to carry "dram-shop" insurance if there is liability imposed on sellers of alcoholic beverages to persons who have already had enough to drink. The restaurant or bar will also have later hours than the rest of the center, which creates additional issues for the shopping center landlord. In addition, some jurisdictions prohibit the sale of liquor within a certain distance of a school or church.

Some specialty retail leases may require variances or special-use permits to comply with zoning. One use that leaps to mind is auto (especially used car) sales that may be specifically addressed in the zoning ordinance.

A bank has special security issues. If the landlord is providing janitorial services, such as in a mixed-use building, the bank will probably want its own people to perform that function, which will affect the operating expense calculation, not only for the bank, but also for the remaining tenants who are served by the janitorial service. A movie theater has special parking requirements and extended hours. It might contain a restaurant and will certainly sell refreshments, which creates problems similar to those of restaurants. Suffice it to say that movie theater leases offer many complications. A health club may require extra floor support for its heavy equipment and it may generate a lot of noise. A day care center has numerous requirements to comply with licensing laws and protection of the children and may also create a noise issue, especially if the children have an outdoor play area.

In mixed-use buildings, the method of allocating taxes, operating expenses, or common area expenses is quite complicated, and the parties may have differing ideas as to what is a fair allocation. There are also issues of access and security that may have to be dealt with.

Ground Lease—Uses

Ground leases are often used when (a) for some reason, the owner of the property cannot or does not want to sell it, but wants some of the benefits from the real estate; (b) the prospective tenant cannot raise the equity to buy the land for its intended use but is able to fund the construction of new improvements on the property; or (c) the landlord wants its property developed and does not have the capital or know-how to do so. The ground lease is thus a form of financing.

Ground leases are much more common in some parts of the country than in others. Those types of leases are much more prevalent in New York, for example, than in the Midwest. They are very useful if the property is appropriate for development or re-development. For example, a piece of land may have had an obsolete strip center on it and be suitable, physically and economically, for a mid-rise office building. The tenant will seek a lease long enough to use up the useful life of the improvement and to obtain the financing to demolish the old structure and construct the new one. Needless to say, the tenant may not undertake to sign a ground lease and construct a building without a firm commitment for a lease or leases (unless it proposes to use the property for its own business). A lease will be a requirement for the tenant to finance the project. Thus, the ground lease will likely be for a minimum term of 40 years, and perhaps for as long as 99 years, either as the primary term or the primary term with options to extend.

Another form of ground lease occurs when a landlord simply leases a vacant lot to a tenant for use as a parking lot or for storage. That situation is more analogous to an industrial/warehouse lease and will not be further considered here.

Some Special Issues Customary in Ground Leases

Since ground leases are, in a sense, a sale of vacant land (since the term is so long and the tenant intends to build new improvements on the property), the tenant will have to approach the leasing as it would a purchase. It will need a due diligence period to determine the suitability of the property for the intended use. It may even make the deal contingent on the execution of a sublease or subleases for a proposed building. Thus, if the tenant is entering into the ground lease because it is negotiating a build and lease deal with, for example, a movie theater, the tenant will want the right to terminate the ground lease if it fails to reach agreement with the prospective theater subtenant.

Needless to say, whether the ground lease involves property with existing improvements or vacant property, if the use is to be changed, the parties and their representatives will be concerned with zoning and will have to confirm that its proposed use and structure will comply.

In addition, the tenant is concerned about protecting its subtenants in the event that the ground lease is terminated for any reason. It will want the lease to provide that the landlord will not terminate non-defaulting subtenants if the ground tenant, as the prime tenant, defaults and the ground lease itself is terminated. It is in the landlord's interest to agree to that because the subtenants will, in all probability, be obligated to pay a much higher rent than the ground tenant, who will have built the building to house the subtenants under the ground lease.

The landlord has special concerns as well. Inasmuch as a default by the tenant will (unless the tenant's mortgagee takes over the lease) put the landlord in possession of the improved property (probably subject to the subleases the tenant has made), the landlord will want some input or at least approval rights as to the improvements the tenant intends to construct on its land.

Since it is feasible for the tenant to obtain financing secured by its lease by means of a leasehold mortgage or a leasehold deed of trust, the tenant will need language in the ground lease that protects its lender against the lease being terminated if the tenant defaults under the ground lease. These protections are quite extensive, including rights and time to cure and the right to a new lease if the ground lease is terminated, either because of the default or because of the bankruptcy of the tenant. The ground lease must have a sufficiently long term (including tenant options to extend) so that there is value in the remaining term for the lender, and the lender will want liberal rights to assign the lease if it finds a buyer for it.

Sometimes the lender under leasehold financing seeks to require that the ground landlord mortgage its fee interest in the property to secure its mortgage.[3] Unless there is some special benefit to the landlord, it is certainly not in the interest of that landlord to place its interest in the property at risk to secure a loan to its tenant.

An additional landlord concern is the amount of the rent. I once represented a tenant at the end of a ground lease of 99 years in downtown Chicago where the rent (payable in gold) was not increased during the term and in which the tenant had a right to a "new lease" for an additional term of 40 years at the end of the 99 years, at an increased but fixed rent. Apparently no one in 1879 considered that there might be inflation. Today, we are more sensitive to the risk of inflation and we build financial escalations into our ground leases.

Everyone "knows" that even if a lease provides for payment in gold, the rent cannot actually be collected in gold, right? Well, that is only partially true. Provided that the ground lease was in existence in 1933, when it became illegal to require payment in gold, the landlord cannot enforce that provision. However, for contracts made after October 1977, gold payment is legal.

---

3. In many states, the borrower delivers a "trust deed" or "deed of trust" to the lender or to a third party in trust for the lender. There are some technical reasons for that under applicable state law, which are not necessary to discuss here. The trust deed or deed of trust has the effect of a mortgage for the purpose under discussion, and in this book, I refer to "mortgage" for convenience.

Let's say someone takes an assignment today of the tenant's interest in an old ground lease (and there are still many 99-year leases in effect) and the effect of the assignment is to terminate the liability of the old tenant under the lease. The assignment will constitute what we lawyers call a "novation." In plain language, it is considered a new lease.[4] Whoops, the requirement for payment in gold is reinstated.

When the lease was made in 1925, or thereabouts, the official United States price for gold was $20.67 per troy ounce. At this time, gold prices fluctuate constantly, but are generally well over $1,000 per troy ounce. So how much more would it cost to buy an equivalent amount of gold to pay the equivalent number of gold coins specified in the lease? I had a deal where I was representing the assignee. It was pure luck that I recalled hearing about a change in the law (it was just a comment I heard in passing, and I was not confronting the issue at the time). Because of that, we structured the deal as a sublease (without the old tenant being released), and the deal went forward without the risk. It is a trap for the unwary and if it is all you remember from reading this book, it may stand you in good stead.

Because the landlord's value in the lease is in the building, it is customarily provided that once the construction of the building is completed, the tenant no longer has personal liability for the performance of the obligations. This is an additional reason the landlord wants input as to the improvements and possibly as to the subtenants. It should be noted that this makes the ground leases pretty freely assignable. That raises a very interesting issue, and one that lawyers should be aware of, since an assignment could cost the assignee a great deal of money, or the tenant/assignor could make a considerable profit. If there is a transfer tax in your jurisdiction, it may apply to the assignment of ground leases.

An important issue to be considered is what happens to the buildings at the end of the term. Generally, the ground lease will provide that the improvements are deemed to be real estate belonging to the tenant (so the tenant may take advantage of depreciation and other benefits of ownership)

---

4. If you are concerned with this, see 216 Jamaica Avenue, LLC v. S&R Playhouse Realty Co., 540 F.3d 433 (6th Cir. 2008).

and that they become the property of the landlord at the end of the term of the ground lease. But does the landlord want them? A building built early in the term of the 99-year lease, or even a 40-year lease, may be totally obsolete and require demolition. Who is to pay for that? On the other hand, what if somewhere in the middle of a 40-year ground lease the tenant demolishes the improvements and erects new, state-of-the art facilities? Perhaps the landlord may want that. Maybe the tenant, with the landlord's consent, has entered into a sublease extending beyond the expiration of the term of the ground lease. Certainly the improvements should not be demolished under those circumstances. Even though the original negotiators of the ground lease may no longer be around when it expires, they must project themselves into the unknown future so that their clients or their clients' successors are not trapped by those problems that they can, at least, anticipate to occur at the end of the ground lease term.

Government Leases

Government leases are a special animal. I had a client who avoided them like the plague. Another client owned office buildings in a state capital and government leases were his bread and butter.

There are actually some advantages to landlords in government leases, particularly federal government leases where collecting rent is assured. The major advantage is that governments need a lot of space, and they need it in good times and bad. The main disadvantage of government leases is that the landlord is subject to the annual appropriation process and the lease may be terminated if no money is appropriated for the agency or for a particular lease.

If the government entity is short of money, as most are, one of two things might happen: First, the government may delay paying its bills, including rents. This presents serious problems with lenders, as you can well understand. Second, the government may downsize its operations and terminate the lease.

Getting a governmental entity to lease a particular space may be a problem because of political pressure to lease another space, even if it is less suitable for the entity's needs. And corruption might get in the way of a deal or may cause a deal to be made, giving rise to adverse publicity or even criminal prosecution of the landlord.

Rent on government leases is typically paid in arrears, which should not be much of a problem if the rent is paid on time. The landlord may have to front the first month's mortgage payment, but that should not be a major deterrent. A more serious problem is that government leases are usually signed on the government's form, and governments are not particularly eager to negotiate changes.

Also, many government agencies are poor housekeepers. When the landlord gets the space back, it may need a lot of fix-up, especially if the agency services many people. For example, a social security office or an unemployment office has a lot of users who may not be very sensitive to the need to help maintain the condition of the premises.

With all the disadvantages, I suppose government leases are better than no leases, so they keep being made. It is just wise to be aware of the problems.

Subleases

Subleases present a dilemma. Subleasing is much more complicated than direct leasing, but pressure exists to create a simple and inexpensive sublease document. A regular lease basically deals with the rights and obligations of only two parties: the landlord and the tenant. In a sublease, the rights and obligations established in the prime lease between the prime landlord and the prime tenant (being the sublandlord) have a substantial and often controlling effect on the deal between the sublandlord and the subtenant. The sublease situation is further complicated by the fact that there is no direct relationship between the prime landlord and the subtenant, and because the subtenant's use is often different from the sublandlord's.

Despite these inherent complications, the parties to a sublease seek that simple document for many reasons. Principally, they may feel that, because the terms of the lease have already been negotiated between the prime landlord and the sublandlord, the parties to the sublease should not have to revisit settled issues. Additionally, the parties may not understand the complexity of the sublease situation. They may feel that it should be a simple matter to transfer the terms pertaining to the occupancy of the premises from the prime lease to a sublease. Especially in sublease situations for a short term, a small area, or both, the parties do not see a justification for dealing at length (and expensively) with complications, particularly if they do not perceive that the complications exist.

Three traditional approaches to the drafting of subleases exist. I call the first the full sublease or the "all-inclusive" approach, the second the "incorporation by reference" approach, and the third the "haphazard approach."

In the all-inclusive approach, the drafter creates an entirely new lease between the sublandlord and the subtenant, using the prime lease as a point of reference. This new lease may track the form of the prime lease, but will allocate among the prime landlord, the sublandlord, and the subtenant all of the benefits and burdens in the prime lease. At some other place in the sublease, the parties may create a mechanism for the enforcement for the subtenant of the prime landlord's obligations. Because no direct relationship exists between the prime landlord and the subtenant, enforcement against the prime landlord will have to be pursued, if at all, by the sublandlord on the subtenant's behalf, and the sublease may include a provision requiring the sublandlord to enforce the provisions of the prime lease for the benefit of the subtenant, usually at the subtenant's expense. The all-inclusive sublease may also be on a completely new form that, apart from its references to the prime lease, does not resemble or track the prime lease at all. While perhaps dealing thoroughly with the issues, this approach will often unnecessarily prolong and complicate negotiations because, in addition to the drafting time required to create the instrument, the form itself may encourage negotiation of provisions that already have been dealt with in the prime lease and that may not be meaningfully altered. I have done such a lease only once in my career.

In the incorporation-by-reference approach, the drafter sets forth the agreements that apply between the sublandlord and the subtenant only; those agreements are the business terms of the sublease. The drafter then incorporates by reference certain sections of the prime lease that are to apply between the sublandlord and the subtenant. The drafter usually states that the references in the prime lease to the "landlord" shall be deemed to be references to the "sublandlord," and likewise that the references in the prime lease to the "tenant" shall be deemed to be references to the "subtenant." The better drafted incorporation-by-reference subleases will qualify those obligations of the prime landlord that are to remain with the prime landlord and those that are to be performed by, or for the benefit of, the sublandlord. As in the all-inclusive approach, some provision is usually made for the enforcement of the obligations of the prime landlord for the benefit of the subtenant. The incorporation-by-reference approach is the one most frequently used, but it is not terribly efficient because the parties have to be certain that the appropriate provisions in the prime lease are incorporated or excluded from the incorporation, and any time the parties have to refer to the terms of the sublease, they may also have to refer to the prime lease, which may be an extremely long and complicated document.

In the haphazard approach, the drafter may pull a lease form from the shelf, name it a "sublease," change the references to identify the parties as "sublandlord" and "subtenant," and use the phrase "hereby subleases" instead of "hereby leases." This type of sublease may have a section prohibiting each party from causing a default under the prime lease, but it does not meaningfully allocate the rights and obligations of the three parties.

Both the all-inclusive approach and the incorporation-by-reference approach have advantages and disadvantages. The haphazard approach has no advantages.

With my friend and colleague, Martin Miner, a partner in the law firm of Holland & Knight in New York, I considered this situation and we proposed an alternative approach—a generic sublease. In a sense, the creation of a generic sublease attempts to accomplish the impossible. It seeks to create a vehicle that will serve in all situations, whether they be office, industrial/warehouse, retail, or even residential. It also seeks to coexist with any prime lease, no matter what the covenants and agreements between the prime landlord and the sublandlord may be. The proposed form attempts to accomplish this by dealing first with the business terms of the sublease transaction and the other agreements that apply solely between the sublandlord and the subtenant and then dealing with issues that are unique to the sublease situation. The business terms and the agreements that apply between the sublandlord and subtenant are typical of any lease situation and do not require further discussion. However, the way that the form deals with the sublease issues does require attention. First, the sublease identifies the prime lease but does not directly incorporate it by reference. Second, the sublease seeks to allocate responsibilities that are the sublandlord's under the prime lease but that are undertaken, in whole or in part, by the subtenant under the sublease. Third, the sublease seeks to prevent the subtenant from doing things not permitted without the prime landlord's consent unless such consent (as well as that of the sublandlord) is obtained. Fourth, it contains a set of provisions that deal directly with a number of the issues that are created in the sublease situation. Finally, it contains provisions that are often inserted in a prime landlord's consent to the sublease.

As to this final point, it should be noted that prime landlords are not particularly shy about seeking benefits when they are asked to consent to a sublease. For example, they might ask for additional security deposits or for other amendments to the prime lease or even the sublease itself, and those requests might impact the sublandlord, the subtenant, or both. If the prime lease provides that consent may not be unreasonably withheld, such conditions to a consent may not really be permissible, but very few tenants have the time, the money, or the inclination to litigate over the matter.[5] Three party discussions may be required to resolve those issues, and it is really impossible to prevent that situation when negotiating the sublease, or even at the time the prime lease is entered into.

It is not my purpose to include any forms in this book. If, however, you want to get a sublease done efficiently, you may refer to the article, "Subleases: A New Approach Revisited," *Real Property, Probate and Trust Journal*, Volume 41, Number 1, Spring 2006, page 1, or to an earlier version of the sublease (and a longer explanation) in the article, "Subleases: A New Approach—A Proposal," *Real Property, Probate and Trust Journal*, Volume 34, Number 1, Spring 1999, page 1. Of course, those forms, like any forms, will have to be modified when used, in order to fit the particulars of the pending deal.

---

5. Some leases provide that consent will not be unreasonably withheld, conditioned, or delayed. That is fine, but if consent is unreasonably conditioned or delayed, is it not also being unreasonably withheld?

Specialty Leases

There are many types of specialty leases and the number and type are probably proliferating as technology changes. Such leases may apply to areas inside, outside, above, or below buildings.

For example, space below a building or an existing parking lot or vacant ground may be suitable for a below-ground parking area. It can readily be seen that such a lease creates issues of support, access, sharing of costs and taxes, as well as many others.

Another example is the "ground" leasing of the space above an existing building for another use. That might arise where a downtown shopping center is purposely built in such a manner as to support a hotel above it, and where the hotel is to be "owned" by a separate entity. That ownership may be a fee ownership in which a so-called "vertical subdivision" is created, or it may be a long term lease, which is analogous to a ground lease but with provisions dealing with issues of support, access for utilities, special elevators, and the like.

A third example is a lease permitting the use of the risers, as well as basement space, to a tenant that is providing communication services to the occupants of the building. Such an arrangement may be in the form of a license that gives provider contractual rights but not a real property interest.

A particularly troubling specialty lease is one that gives the tenant the right to construct a communications tower or other facility on the landlord's property. That tower or facility may be located on the building itself, on the ground level of improved property, or on unimproved property. The improvements to be constructed by the tenant may be expensive, or the precise location may be critical, or both. In either case, the tenant usually presents a draft lease to the landlord, and it is often very one-sided. The term may be long, the rent minimal (particularly in the case of facility on top of an existing building); the lease may include the right to run lines through the building risers and the use of a small amount of space in the basement for equipment; and the tenant, but not the landlord, may have the right to terminate the lease.

Lease Provisions Common to Most Leases

4

I admit that I approach this section with some trepidation. I have read lease provision analyses and they are usually as dry as dust. I hope that is not my style of writing. I shall do my best to make this section as readable as the prior ones so that the information presented is not just reference material, but an enjoyable read. Here is how I propose to handle this material. First, I shall discuss, in no particular order, a number of provisions common to most types of leases. When I shall have sufficiently whetted your appetite, I will delve into provisions that are specific to certain types of leases. Here goes!

The Parties

Landlord

Who is the landlord, anyway? You, as the tenant's lawyer, should ask yourself, "Is the landlord a party that could possibly default in its mortgage and put my tenant client in trouble? Will my client actually collect the promised allowance for tenant improvements? Does the landlord named in the lease really own the property?"

The answers to those questions are important, but chances are you will not really find out the identity of the principals of the landlord. The landlord will usually be an entity, such as a limited liability company, created to limit the owners' exposure. In some states, land trusts are still in use, but even if they are not, the property may be in an active trust or a corporation. If a limited liability company is the owner and it is member-managed, you will be able to find the identity of the members, but if it is manager-managed, you will only find the identity of the manager. The member or the manager may, in fact, be another entity. Even if the property is beneficially owned by an individual or a family, the title may still be in some entity.

The landlord's actual ownership of the property is not a common risk, but the only sure way for a tenant to protect itself is to obtain leasehold title insurance (see page 86). However, that insurance is most typically obtained in situations where an entire property is being leased (as in a ground lease) or the lease is for a major space.

It is the payment of the tenant allowance or other concessions that is one of the more serious issues for the tenant. The payment might be coming out of loan proceeds, but there are two risks there. First, the lender might not be solvent. Second, the landlord might default and give the lender a basis not to fund the allowance.

In this situation, there are a couple of ways the tenant can protect itself. It can insist on a right of set-off against rent if the allowance is not paid. That is not a perfect solution because it means that the tenant will have to advance the payment for the improvements (which it may not be able to finance) and only later get it back by savings in rent payments. Alternatively, the tenant may ask the landlord to provide security for the payment, preferably in the form of a letter of credit from a substantial bank.

Tenant

Similar questions and issues arise in connection with the identity of the tenant. Is the tenant under the lease an entity that actually exists? Is it a separate entity or a division of another entity? Does the financial data provided give an accurate description of the financial position of the entity that is to be the tenant?

Let us assume that the proposed tenant is a major company known as ABC, Inc., that you represent the landlord, and that the tenant proposes a lease in which the named tenant is not ABC, Inc., but is ABC Company.

First, you as the lawyer for the landlord can look up the records of the sec-retary of state where the tenant is said to be incorporated (or organized, if it is a limited liability company). You may find that it is listed, but if you don't find it, you may be advised by the tenant's lawyer that it is really a "division" of ABC, Inc. A division of an entity is not a separate entity and does not ordinarily have the legal authority to sign leases or other contracts. The tenant should really be ABC, Inc., but you are told that the authorized officers of ABC, Inc. do not sign division leases for premises of this size.

Next, you ask for a corporate resolution from ABC, Inc.'s board of direc-tors authorizing the division officers to sign the lease. You are told that none exists, but at the next meeting in three weeks, one may be passed, but probably won't be. You want the lease to be made, and you are "assured" by the tenant that there will be no problem, that other landlords have signed leases with this "entity." In fact, you are the only one who has ever questioned it (this is to try to make you feel bad or foolish, but you should really feel proud that you have raised a real and material issue). Once the tenant moves in, it cannot say that it was not authorized because there will have been substantial part performance by the tenant in accepting delivery of the space by the landlord, and substantial part performance binds the tenant even if the person signing the lease was not authorized to do so. On the other hand, it could be a major problem if the landlord is being called upon to do substantial build-out, which will take considerable time, during which the tenant may say that the division was not authorized to sign the lease, that its acts were what we lawyers call "ultra vires," or beyond the signer's power, and therefore not binding. I have no easy answer for this one. It becomes the landlord's business call.

Let's change the facts a little. Let us assume that ABC Company is not a division of ABC, Inc., but its subsidiary. A subsidiary is a separate entity and has authority to sign leases. Good! The landlord asks for a financial statement and is promptly sent an annual report—of ABC, Inc. Where is the financial statement of ABC Company? There is none. ABC, Inc.'s annual report, which contains its current financial statements, is a consolidated statement of ABC, Inc., its subsidiaries, and divisions. There is no state-ment for ABC Company, but that is the tenant, not ABC, Inc. Does ABC Company have the wherewithal to perform its obligations under the lease?

You don't know. You may request whatever financial data is available for ABC Company, but it may be pretty sketchy. Will ABC, Inc. guaranty the obligations under the lease? Maybe it will, or maybe it won't. Will ABC Company put up a substantial security deposit? Maybe it will, or maybe it won't. Another business call.

All right, you have convinced ABC, Inc. to sign the lease for ABC Company as its division. You receive the lease and it is signed by the division president. That is another problem. What authority does the division president have to bind ABC, Inc. to the lease, even one for that division? Only the president of a corporation (not a division president) or the manager of an LLC, has *apparent* authority to sign leases or other contracts. You ask for a corporate resolution but get the same answer as before—none exists and none is likely to exist. Business call again.

Insurance

Insurance is kind of a wilderness for many lawyers. Many of us simply do not know enough about it, so we pass the responsibility for the review of the language to insurance agents or risk managers. While it is a good idea for a lawyer representing a landlord to have a knowledgeable insurance expert review the language when it is drafted into the lease form, it does not often happen. That is why many leases still refer to "comprehensive liability insurance" when the real name, other than for automobile insurance, is "commercial liability insurance"; or why leases have low insurance amounts or have different amounts for personal injury and for property damage; when policies are now written with a combined single limit; or why leases still refer to the National Board of Underwriters, which has not existed since the 1930s.[1]

---

1. I have developed a non-conventional "no fault" (really "less fault") approach to insurance provisions in my lease forms, which I have been using for several years. While I often get push-back on the concept, when it is understood, it is generally accepted. You can learn more about it in my Article "Allocation of Insurable Risks in Commercial Leases" published in the *Real Property, Probate and Trust Journal*, Volume 37, Number 3 at page 479 (Fall 2002). It is available free to ABA members, accessible at the following website: http://www.americanbar

The following is a primer on the treatment of insurable risks in commercial leases. Although rather long, I hope you find it useful.

It is always a good idea for the lawyer representing the tenant to have the tenant's insurance person review the insurance-related provisions to confirm that the tenant has or will be able to get the required coverage. It should be noted that there are more sections in the lease that are insurance impacted than the one labeled "Insurance." Those include the sections pertaining to waiver of claims, waiver of the right of subrogation, indemnities, and fire and casualty, all of which are discussed below.

Simply stated, leases must deal with three insurance issues:

- Who causes what loss to whom or to whose property?
- Who has the ultimate liability for the loss?
- Whose insurance is going to pay for it?

Every landlord's lease form deals with those issues and every tenant wishes to minimize its own risk.

Liability arises when one party injures another or damages the other's property, usually as a result of some sort of fault such as negligence or deliberate misconduct. Liability is imposed to compensate the victim for the loss or damage occasioned by that wrongful act. The most common form of liability arises out of automobile accidents, but the real estate professional is aware that the issue often arises when a person slips and falls on real estate or when personal property is damaged as a result of such things as falling ceiling tiles or leaking roofs.

A property loss occurs as a result of a casualty that causes the damage or destruction of property, real or personal. A common type of such a casualty is fire, but damage caused by high winds or other natural occurrences is also a casualty loss.

Businesses purchase property insurance to create a source of funds from which to recover for property damage resulting from a casualty;[2] they also carry separate liability insurance (frequently with different insurance companies) to provide a defense and funds that they can use to pay third parties for losses that they caused. Although they tend to think that these two sorts of risks are not interrelated, the loss arising from a casualty that is caused by the negligence or other fault of one party and causes a loss to a second party may be insured both by the liability coverage of the party at fault and by the property insurance of the injured party.

For example, assume that a building owner is inspecting the roof and drops a cigarette, causing a fire that damages the tenant's merchandise or machinery and equipment. The loss is covered by the building owner's liability insurance but may also be covered by the tenant's contents insurance, which is a form of property insurance. Conversely, if the tenant's employee throws a lighted match into a wastebasket and causes the building to be substantially damaged by fire, the damage is covered by the landlord's property insurance on the building and may also be covered by the tenant's liability insurance.

If both parties carry property insurance and liability insurance, why is it necessary for the lease to deal with insurance issues at all? Or, why should the lease not provide that the party at fault bears the loss and, to the extent that the loss is not covered by liability insurance, the property insurance of the other party pays the balance? The relevant provisions of many leases deal with the risks in just this way; but this arrangement is not the most economical way to deal with those risks, nor is it necessarily in the best interest of either party.

The basic problem relates to limits on the proceeds of insurance policies. Property insurance typically is tied in some way to the value of the

---

2. Insurance professionals and real estate professionals have a nomenclature problem. Real estate professionals tend to refer to risks involving "fire and other casualty" as "casualty" risks and refer to "property damage" as a liability issue (as in "personal injury and property damage"). Insurance professionals use the word *casualty* to refer to an occurrence causing damage and define insurance covering "fire or other casualty" as "property insurance." I will use the insurance companies' terminology, referring to "property insurance", "liability insurance", and where appropriate, "property damage liability insurance."

property, whereas liability insurance is purchased with a somewhat arbitrarily determined maximum level. Until several years ago, it was typical to carry liability insurance for damage to property in an amount of only between $250,000 and $500,000 per occurrence. Today, the insured customarily obtains a personal injury and property damage liability policy with a combined single limit of, for example, $3 million. Substantial excess liability (or "umbrella") coverage with higher limits may also be purchased.

Thus, if the tenant's employee (in the second example) caused a building with a replacement cost of $50 million to be totally destroyed, the landlord's property insurance, if purchased with at least that insurance limit, would be obligated to pay the entire loss. But the parties would discover that if the tenant's property damage liability insurance were applied to the loss, the maximum amount of recovery is the policy limit, which probably is substantially less than $50 million. Similarly, the destruction of extremely valuable machinery and equipment (computer equipment or very costly merchandise) as a result of the landlord's negligence might not be adequately covered by the landlord's property damage liability insurance.

A further complication is the fact that, under common law, any person causing damage by his negligence or other wrongful act has liability for the damage, whether or not he has liability insurance to cover that loss. Thus, in the example in which the tenant's employee caused the building to burn down, the landlord has the right to sue the tenant (the tenant is liable for the negligent act of its employee performed in the course of his or her employment) whether or not the tenant has liability insurance and whether or not that insurance provides coverage or is adequate.

In fact, if the landlord's property insurance carrier pays the landlord for the loss of the building, the insurance carrier has the right under common law to sue the tenant (the party at fault) to recover the amount that it paid to the landlord. The right of the insurance company to "stand in the shoes" of its insured and to bring the insured's negligence claim against the party at fault is called a "right of subrogation."[3] Whether the lawsuit is brought by

---

3. *Subrogation* and *subordination* (see page 73) may sound the same, but they are different and unrelated. Do not become confused.

the landlord or the landlord's insurance company, it could result in liability imposed upon the tenant for an amount far in excess of the tenant's liability insurance coverage. Obviously, the same principles apply in the example in which the landlord's negligence caused the extensive loss to the tenant.

You can see that it is in the interest of each party to have losses arising out of the damage or destruction of their property paid by a property insurance carrier and somehow to negate both the right to action of the party owning the damaged property and the right of subrogation of that party's property insurance carrier. Both of these ends can, with some limitations, be accomplished in the lease. I recommend the following three-pronged approach:

1. First, each party should be required to carry property insurance with appropriate coverage and appropriate amounts (see the following discussion);
2. second, each party should waive its right to claims for damage to its property arising out of the negligence or wrongful act of the other party; and
3. finally, each party should agree to obtain from its insurance carrier a waiver of the right of subrogation. The waiver of subrogation might, in fact, be evidenced by a provision in the insurance policy that the coverage is not invalidated by reason of the fact that the insured has, prior to a loss, waived its right to proceed against a party at fault causing the damage or destruction of the property insured by the policy.

These three requirements—insurance coverage, waiver of claims, and waiver of subrogation rights—go a long way toward eliminating fault as the basis for paying for damage or destruction of property and limit coverage of that risk to the property insurance of the party owning the property.

Waiver of Claims and Waiver of Subrogation

Many leases contain specific provisions to the effect that the tenant waives claims against the landlord for property damage. It is not as common that there are such specific provisions for the benefit of the tenant. On the other hand, most (but certainly not all) waivers of subrogation provisions are mutual and protect each party. A mutual waiver of subrogation provision, to be effective, should also contain a waiver of claims and provide for a waiver of subrogation so long as such protection is available from insurance carriers, plus provisions for notice if such a benefit is either not available or is available only at additional cost. The right of the insured to waive (prior to a loss) the right of subrogation is now common in the insurance industry. As a rule, insurance companies make such waivers generally available because their premiums are based on risk factors that do not include an anticipation of recovery of the proceeds of the insurance from a third party. In other words, property insurers do not think they will be able to recover from third parties (whose identity may not even be known), so they calculate the insured's premium on the assumption that no such recovery will be possible.

Sometimes language drafted into the lease is evenhanded and is generally acceptable to both landlords and tenants. However, some waiver of claims provisions and mutual waiver of subrogation provisions contain unacceptable and dangerous language, because they deal with matters other than property damage, or they do not sufficiently eliminate fault from the allocation of risk. For example, waivers of claims provisions frequently refer to "injury to persons." They are asking the tenant to waive claims for personal injury as well as property damage, even though personal injury is not a risk compensated by the tenant's property insurance. This is unfair to injured persons because it may deprive them of the right to recover damages. Tenants should reject a waiver of claims for personal injury in a lease.[4] Many jurisdictions have statutes or case law that state that such waivers of claims of personal injury are void as against public policy.

Some waivers of subrogation are, unfortunately, not *mutual* waivers. Sometimes landlord-prepared forms require the tenant to waive claims against the landlord, and they require the tenant's insurance carrier to waive its right of subrogation against the landlord; however, they contain no reciprocal landlord agreements for the benefit of the tenant. Some waivers of

---

4. If the tenant is an entity, the waiver by that entity does not bind the employees of that entity who are injured. Even if the tenant is a live person, the waiver for personal injury would affect only that person and not his or her employees. For that reason, landlords may require an indemnity, which is discussed below (see page 52).

subrogation provide that the waiver applies only to the extent of *collectible* insurance proceeds. This is a substantial limit on the benefits of the waiver if the party that owns the damaged property has no property insurance or inadequate property insurance (or if it gave the insurance carrier a defense against the payment of insurance proceeds, for example, by making false statements when it procured the insurance).

Thus, the waiver of subrogation should apply to the extent of the other party's property insurance (which should be described and should be adequate to cover possible losses). If, for example, the lease requires the landlord to carry property insurance on a full replacement cost basis (see page 47), the waiver should apply to the extent of insurance required to be carried. If, however, the lease does not expressly require the landlord to carry such insurance, the waiver should apply to an amount of proceeds that the landlord would have recovered if so-called "all-risk" (really "Special Form") property insurance were carried on a full replacement cost basis without coinsurance (see explanation on page 47). Obviously, the same principle applies regarding the tenant's insurance. Nearly all leases require the tenant to insure its contents. Not as many require the landlord to insure its property.

Appropriate provision should also be made in the event that the party owning the property carries a large deductible or self-insures for a property loss. In that case, to the extent the party self-insures, that self-insurance should be deemed to be "insurance" for the purpose of the waiver of claims and of subrogation.

In short, the waiver of claims and the waiver of subrogation should eliminate fault as a factor in connection with the payment for a loss and place the risk on the party that owns the property who is in the position to carry property insurance.[5]

The amounts and kinds of property insurance to be required should vary with the nature of the insured property. The lease should discuss the following matters:

---

5. The property owner may contract with the other party to carry the property insurance. This occurs when a net lease requires the tenant to purchase the property insurance on the building.

- Contents insurance
- Property insurance on the building
- Proceeds available to rebuild
- Rent insurance
- Other insurance issues

Contents Insurance

Optimally, the lease should require the tenant to insure all contents, trade fixtures, machinery, equipment, furniture, and furnishings in the premises on a replacement cost basis under Special Form coverage insurance. "Special Form" coverage insures what used to be known as "all-risk" insurance, which was confusing because it did not really cover all risks, but every risk except for certain excluded risks, which were specified in the policy. In other words, it was not all-risk insurance after all.

In a lease that contains waivers of claims and mutual waivers of subrogation rights, the landlord wants this clause to ensure that the tenant has adequate insurance on its own property. If the tenant is actually carrying the required insurance and collects for any insured loss from its own insurance carrier, it has no economic reason to bring an action against the landlord even if the loss arises from the landlord's negligence; meanwhile, the waiver of the right of subrogation protects the landlord from suit by the tenant's insurance carrier.

Property Insurance on the Building

In a multi-tenant building, the landlord customarily carries the building's property insurance, whereas in a single-tenant building, the tenant sometimes carries the building insurance, naming the landlord as the insured.

When the landlord does carry the insurance in industrial/warehouse buildings, it pays the premium and usually passes all or some of the cost to its tenants. In office buildings and in shopping centers, the cost of building insurance is typically an "operating expense," or a "common area charge" that is also passed through, in whole or in part, to the tenants. The building coverage may be broad or narrow; it may include only standard fire and extended coverage insurance, or it may include Special Form coverage.

If the tenant is obligated under the lease to repair or restore following damage or destruction of the building (which is not unusual in ground leases and other net leases of a fairly long duration), the lease customarily provides that the proceeds needed for rebuilding will be made available to the tenant. If the tenant is not obligated to rebuild, the lease will generally specify the conditions under which a landlord must do so. It should be noted that, in either event, the landlord's mortgage may provide that the lender has the right to apply insurance proceeds to pay down the indebtedness, rather than to make the proceeds available to rebuild.

Tenant Improvements and Alterations

Often the landlord insures the entire building, including leasehold improvements and tenant alterations. On the other hand, it is not unusual for the landlord to insure only the shell and core of the building, and the tenant to be required to insure its own leasehold improvements and alterations. In my judgment, it is better for both parties (and certainly for the landlord's mortgagee) if the landlord undertakes to rebuild the entire building to its prior condition, and insures on that basis. However I have learned that, especially in situations where tenant improvements are substantial, such as in retail leases, the landlord's insurance actually covers only the shell and core of the building and the tenant is required by the lease to insure its improvements and alterations, notwithstanding the fact that the landlord is, most likely, required by its mortgage to insure the building as improved because the lender does not want to have to chase a number of tenants to get the insurance proceeds so it can systematically make them available to rebuild.

The tenant is paying for the landlord's property insurance, either in its base rent or in additional rent. Thus, if the landlord is insuring the building as improved (as required by its mortgage) and the tenant is required to carry property insurance on its alterations or leasehold improvements, the tenant is paying twice for the same insurance, which is in neither party's interest. In that situation, when I represent landlords, I get the "Taj Mahal" argument. Why, the tenant questions, should all the tenants pay their pro rata share of the cost of the insurance if a particular tenant spends an enormous sum to improve its space? There are two answers to that. Unless it is the major tenant, the cost of the insurance will probably not increase that much. If there is a substantial increase in the cost of the insurance, however, the landlord should (and usually will) require that the tenant with the expensive improvements pay the increase as a condition the landlord's consenting to the improvement. Since most tenants will not ordinarily negotiate to share in the benefit of other tenants paying a greater share of the landlord's insurance cost, the landlord will, in all probability, not reduce the other tenants' share of the cost of insurance, so the landlord may double dip (keeping the excess for itself) which is, of course, unfair to the other tenants. In any case, the "Taj Mahal" situation is an unusual occurrence

Proceeds Available to Rebuild

Unfortunately, this is an area that does not receive much attention until after a fire or other insurable casualty has actually occurred. Leases typically require that the landlord's insurance proceeds be payable to the landlord, subject to a standard mortgage clause in the event that the premises are mortgaged to secure the landlord's indebtedness. The standard mortgage clause requires the insurance company to pay the proceeds to the lender. Whether the lender makes the insurance proceeds available so that the landlord (or the tenant, if so provided in the lease) can rebuild the premises depends on the terms of the mortgage. The first draft of most mortgages provides that if there is a fire or other casualty, the proceeds are to be paid to the lender, who may then apply the proceeds to pay down the loan or to restore the property. (It is beyond the scope of this book, but I strongly argue that the lender should, in most cases, be obligated to make the proceeds available to restore, and that should be dealt with when the loan commitment is being negotiated.)

If a proposed lease is to be in place before the building is mortgaged, the parties to the lease, and their lawyers, should make sure that the mortgage will provide that the insurance proceeds will be made available to rebuild—provided, of course, that the lease remains in full force and effect. That is easier said than done, since the mortgage may not be negotiated until some time after the lease is signed and the lawyers have, by then, moved on to other deals. In that situation, however, the lawyers should educate their clients so that when the landlord mortgages the property, it will be alerted to the issue, and when the tenant is asked to sign a Subordination, Non-Disturbance and Attornment Agreement (see page 106), it can seek to negotiate a provision in that Agreement to the effect that the proceeds will be made available to rebuild the tenant's premises. Obviously, the tenant may need some economic clout to get such a provision, but that is the only time it may get the relief it requires.

If the mortgage is in place before the lease is signed, the tenant's lawyer should review the mortgage to determine if that document provides for the proceeds to be made available. If it does not, and if again the tenant has sufficient economic clout, it can make the lease conditioned on obtaining a Non-Disturbance Agreement that will require the lender to make the proceeds available to rebuild, subject to customary conditions (such as the landlord's not being in default under the loan documents or there being enough time left in the term of the loan, or the landlord's making up any shortfall in the insurance proceeds). If the protection required by the tenant is not forthcoming, the tenant should seek the right to terminate the lease before any money is spent on construction of the tenant's improvements.

If the lender has not agreed in the loan documents or, as to a particular tenant in a Non-Disturbance Agreement, to make the proceeds available to rebuild, and if the landlord cannot obtain such an agreement at the time of a casualty, the landlord should have a right to terminate its tenant leases (otherwise, it would be in default under the leases). However, the tenant may not get a comparable right to terminate.

It is critically important to the landlord that tenants not be able to terminate their leases merely because of a fire or other casualty. If the leases are terminated, the lenders will certainly not make the insurance proceeds available for the rebuilding of the property (and that will no doubt be stated in the loan documents as an exception to the lender's obligation to make them available). The landlord would then be in an untenable position, especially if the building is only partly damaged. In that case, any proceeds that the landlord receives would probably not be enough to pay off the loan, the debt service payment obligation would continue without reduction or abatement, and the landlord would have little or no income from which to service the debt. He would have to go into the mortgage market, possibly in a higher interest rate market, with a half-destroyed building, to borrow funds to pay off the old debt and to rebuild the building so that he can re-lease it on a speculative basis. Of course, the tenant should be able to terminate if the landlord defaults in its obligation to rebuild (or to make the proceeds available to the tenant to rebuild if the tenant is obligated to do the restoration) or if the lender does not make the proceeds available.

Rent Insurance

The party that purchases the property insurance can, for a reasonable additional premium, buy coverage that will pay continuing expenses (like rent and taxes) during the period that the premises are untenantable (which means unfit for the purpose for which they are leased). If the lease is a net lease in which the rent is not abated, the insurance proceeds will not be paid. If the lease is silent on rent abatement, the tenant's lawyer should find out whether rent insurance proceeds will be paid, because the law in most states provides that rent will not abate in that case. In those states, rent abates only if the lease expressly provides for abatement. If rent does not abate, either because the lease so provides or because there is no provision in the lease and the law of the state is that it does not, then the insurance company will probably assert that there is no loss to the landlord and accordingly that there should be no proceeds of rent loss insurance. If, however, the rent does abate as a result of the fire or other casualty, the landlord must be certain that it receives insurance proceeds that will permit it to continue to pay debt service and taxes.

Many leases provide that rent does not abate if the tenant caused the loss. If that is the case, the insurance company may have a defense to paying the proceeds of the rent loss insurance. Such a provision is intended to punish the tenant, but it does not really benefit the landlord. It only benefits the insurance company, which does not have to pay a claim for which it was actually compensated in its premium. If the tenant does not have business interruption insurance (actually called "business income insurance"), the tenant will likely be unable to pay the rent while it is out of business because of the loss. Thus, a provision that says rent does not abate if the tenant caused the loss makes no sense at all since it punishes the landlord as well as the tenant, and perhaps even more than the tenant.

Business Income Insurance

If all or a part of the premises are rendered untenantable and the lease does not terminate, the tenant may be forced to move out of the premises, move into other premises on a temporary basis, set up its operation and pay rent there, and then move out of the other premises and reoccupy the original premises when the repair or restoration is completed. If the rent does not abate, the tenant will continue to have to pay the rent as well. All of that will, of course, involve considerable expense, and the tenant may cover business interruption and extra expenses by means of so-called "business income insurance." Most leases are silent about tenants' business income insurance. Tenants may argue, in negotiating for a right to terminate, that moving out and moving back in involves tremendous inconvenience and trauma, but the landlord's response must be that both landlord and tenant suffer from a casualty and that, so long as the economic loss can be covered by business income insurance, the tenant should not have a right to terminate the lease. The problem of the retail tenant is more difficult than the problem of other tenants because comparable store premises may simply not be available in the same market. However, tenants can insure against loss of profits.

Loss Payable Provision

Occasionally, when the lease requires the tenant to carry the building property insurance, the tenant may seek to negotiate that insurance proceeds be payable to both parties "as their interest may appear." However, the proceeds of the building property insurance should be payable only to the landlord. After all, the landlord does own the building. If the landlord is having a dispute with the tenant, it does not want to be required to get the tenant's endorsement on the insurance proceeds check. Likewise, the tenant wants to be certain that the landlord's signature is not required on the check for its contents insurance proceeds.

If the tenant is required to rebuild leasehold improvements or alterations, and to insure them separately, it may want to be a payee of the insurance check for those items. On the other hand, the installed leasehold improvements do belong to the landlord, and they are subject to the lien of the landlord's mortgage. In that situation, the tenant's insurance should include a standard mortgage clause. I have serious issues with provisions in leases that require tenants to insure their leasehold improvements and alterations, which was discussed below (see page 42).

Adjustment of Loss

It takes considerable time to adjust the loss after a fire or other casualty in a commercial building. The loss may be adjusted by the insurance carrier or by a public adjuster; it may be contested and involve lengthy disputes. Until the adjustment process is almost completed, the party obligated to rebuild does not know the extent of the proceeds available to rebuild and accordingly cannot make binding commitments. Once it can start planning, it must have plans and specifications drawn and find and negotiate with a contractor to perform the work.

Many leases give the party required to rebuild 60 days to accomplish the necessary steps prior to the commencement of the repair or rebuilding. That is an extremely short time for the landlord to adjust the loss, have the reconstruction designed, hire contractors, and be prepared to start construction. On the other hand, tenants who may be out of business argue for the shortest possible time, and that is how it often ends up.

Replacement Cost, Actual Cash Value, and Coinsurance

If someone insures a building for its actual cash value (sometimes referred to as "insurable value"), the insurance proceeds are limited to the building's replacement cost at the time of the loss, minus physical depreciation (usually estimated at 1% for each year of the building's age). Assume that a 20-year-old building with a replacement cost of $10 million is insured for that amount on an actual cash value basis and is totally destroyed. The insurance carrier may assert that the physical depreciation is 20 percent or $2 million and that the net proceeds of the insurance are limited to $8 million. Obviously, this leaves the landlord with less than he needs to rebuild the building.

If, however, the insurance is written on a full replacement cost basis, the insurer makes no deduction for physical depreciation, and the insured is entitled to receive the full cost of replacement (provided the insured has accurately estimated and purchased coverage for the actual replacement cost and subject, of course, to deductibles).

Many policies are written with 100% coinsurance clauses. That means that the insurance company pays 100 % of the loss (assuming, again, that the amount of insurance carried is enough to pay the loss and that the insurance is carried on a replacement cost basis). This is appropriate if the insured has not underestimated the replacement cost. If the insured is carrying less insurance than is required to replace the building, not only would the underinsuring insurance buyer collect less than the building's replacement cost in the case of a total destruction, but he would collect less than the actual cost of repairing in the event of a partial destruction.

Here is how it works: If an owner insures the same $10 million building for $6 million at 100 percent coinsurance on a replacement cost basis and the building is totally destroyed, the insurance company is obligated to pay only the face amount of the policy. If, however, the loss is a partial rather than a total loss, the insurance company would pay only 60 percent of the actual loss because the owner's insurance was only 60 percent of the replacement cost. The insurance company would pay only $600,000 of a $1 million loss, even though that payment is significantly less than the $6 million face amount of the policy.

An insurance buyer can avoid the coinsurance problem by purchasing a policy with an "agreed amount endorsement." This endorsement is not a confirmation by the insurance company that the amount of the insurance is adequate. It is merely an agreement by the insurance company that the coinsurance result described above will not apply and that the insurance company will pay 100 percent of any partial loss, provided it is not in excess of the face amount of the policy. Obviously, such an endorsement is important to both parties to a lease.

To reduce the likelihood of underinsurance, it may be appropriate to provide in the lease for a periodic insurance appraisal. That provision should also specify who is obligated to pay for the appraisal.

Uninsured Risks

Although it is possible to insure against most casualty risks, certain risks, such as flood and earthquake, are not covered by Special Form policies. If a property is in a flood-risk area, flood insurance is usually available through an agency of the United States government. Earthquake insurance, on the other hand, may either be unavailable or may be very expensive, even in low-earthquake-risk areas. Unless there is a specific exclusion in the lease, the party obligated under the lease to rebuild following a casualty has contractually obligated himself to rebuild, even in the event of an uninsured casualty. That should certainly be considered in the negotiations.

Liability Insurance

Most liability situations in real estate do not arise because an act by one party to the lease results in damage to property of the other party. Those situations are covered by the waiver of claims and waiver of the right of subrogation discussed above (see page 38). Liability situations usually arise because some real person is injured or because a third party's property is damaged. Injury or damage can occur within the premises or in a common area. To avoid the risk of not suing the right party, the injured party customarily asserts a claim or files suit against all the persons having an interest in the property. To prevent gaps in insurance coverage that may result in liability being imposed on an uninsured party, the system of requiring insurance naming another party as an additional insured has evolved. Still, because of the substantial problems that may arise if an injury to a person is not covered by insurance, the parties frequently duplicate insurance, especially in a multi-tenant building.

In a single-occupant building in which the tenant also has the exclusive use and occupancy of the parking lot and the balance of the real estate, the tenant's liability insurance should cover the entire property, and the landlord may decide not to carry liability insurance at all. If the landlord does carry this insurance, its cost probably would be reduced because it would be considered secondary rather than primary coverage. In multi-tenant buildings, landlords should carry liability insurance because injuries occurring in the common areas may not be covered by the tenant's liability insurance unless they result from the tenant's acts. Of course, each party should carry liability insurance covering its own acts off the property.

Additional or Named Insured

Landlords' lease forms customarily require the tenant to carry liability insurance that names the landlord (as well as the landlord's mortgagee) as an additional insured for injuries to persons or damage to property that occur on the premises themselves. This can generally be achieved without the payment of additional premiums, presumably because the tenant has exclusive control of the premises and because if negligence is involved, it will be the tenant's rather than the landlord's. Thus, if a person is injured on or about the premises, the tenant's liability insurance will respond to that loss, whether it is caused by the landlord or the tenant.

"Additional insured" should not be confused with "named insured." While there is some question (due to judicial decisions) about the scope of the coverage for the landlord if it is included in the tenant's policy as an "additional insured," it is clear that if the landlord is a "named insured" it is actually one of the parties that is covered by the insurance provided for in the policy. While the landlord who is a named insured is jointly liable with the tenant for the payment of the premium, the lease will provide that the tenant must pay for the coverage. Most tenants strongly object to including the landlord as a "named insured," particularly tenants that have policies covering more than one location. Still, it is sometimes agreed to in single-tenant buildings because the tenant will not have to pay for its own liability insurance and for a separate policy for the landlord's liability insurance.

Insurance Limits

Leases customarily specify the amount of liability insurance that the tenant must carry. The required amounts have increased over the years. Given the phenomenon of rising judgments, at some point during the term of a long or extended lease, the specified amount may prove inadequate. A well-drafted lease, therefore, gives the landlord the right, on notice, to require the tenant to increase the liability insurance limits if, in the landlord's reasonable judgment, the specified amount is insufficient to protect the various parties. This requirement protects the tenant as well as the landlord, although it does place the decision in the landlord's hands, to which the tenant or its lawyer may object. An alternative is to relate required amounts of liability insurance to amounts customarily carried in the geographic area. It is not wise to tie increases in liability insurance coverage to increases in the Consumer Price Index because changes in that index are not necessarily related to increases in judgment amounts.

Combined Single Limit Per Occurrence/Aggregate

Liability insurance used to be written with separate amounts for personal injury to one person, for personal injury to more than one person in one occurrence, and for property damage. Now liability insurance is written on the basis of a combined single limit per occurrence and aggregate. This means that there is one limit for the sum of all claims, demands, or actions that arise in a single occurrence, whether those claims, demands, or actions arise out of personal injury or property damage.

The word *aggregate* that the insurance companies tack on to the end of the policy description means that they will not pay more than the aggregate limit in any one policy year. For example, a policy may be written with a $1 million occurrence limit and a $2 million aggregate. If there were three losses of $800,000 each during the policy year, the insurance company would pay only $400,000 toward the third loss. It is possible to obtain an endorsement that specifies that "aggregate" shall apply separately to each location owned or rented by the tenant. It is obviously in the interest of both landlord and tenant to obtain such an endorsement whenever the tenant has more than one location so that no risk is left uncovered.

Occurrence and Claims-Made Coverage

Yet another wrinkle arises from time to time in connection with liability policies. A change in general liability coverage has been imported by the insurance industry from products liability and malpractice coverage. Although it is not common, liability coverage is occasionally written on a claims-made rather than on an occurrence basis. In the occurrence basis situation, a claim is covered if the loss occurred while the policy was in effect, even if the claim is made after the policy expires. A claims-made policy provides coverage only for claims made while the policy is in effect, even if the events on which the claims are based occurred before the particular policy was purchased.

Liability insurance written on a claims-made rather than on an occurrence basis can cause gaps in coverage. Assume, for example, that someone is injured on the premises during the last year of the lease term. The tenant moves out at the end of the term and does not continue to maintain claims-made liability insurance, because it is going out of business.[6] The injured party sues the landlord and tenant after the lease term ends. The tenant's liability insurance no longer covers the loss because the claim was made after the term of the insurance expired. Unfortunately, in this situation, the landlord's problem would not be solved by a provision in the lease requiring the tenant to continue to carry liability insurance on a claims-made basis after the lease has expired. Even if the tenant remains in business, there is no efficient way for the landlord to police or to enforce that obligation.

Most tenants who carry insurance on a claims-made basis are large companies that own or lease numerous properties. Although such large companies are likely to remain in business and to continue to carry insurance on a claims-made basis until after the statute-of-limitation period has expired to cover incidents that occurred during the lease term, the landlord has no assurance that this will be the case. The only way a landlord can adequately protect itself in this situation is to carry its own liability insurance. There is, obviously, a cost in doing that, and landlords expect tenants to bear the cost. It is doubtful that tenants would agree.

Indemnity

Another way for parties to a lease to protect themselves from liability for injuries to persons or damage to property is by the use of indemnities. Leases typically require tenant indemnities to protect the landlord. Liability insurance policies usually contain "contractual liability" language. That means the policy covers liability assumed by the tenant under the lease for injury to persons or damage to the property of others, provided the assumption of liability occurs before the injury or damage. An indemnity, unlike the insurance, is not usually limited in amount; thus, the tenant is assuming

---

6. If the tenant is continuing in business elsewhere, it will most likely be continuing the insurance coverage, which is fine, unless the tenant switches to occurrence insurance; going out of business is the major risk for landlords.

liability to pay a judgment against the landlord that might be greater than the coverage required in the lease or the amount of the tenant's actual liability insurance limits (if greater than what the lease requires). Indemnities frequently cover more than liability claims. They may relate to claims for damages arising out of the failure of the tenant to perform other obligations of the tenant under the lease. Insurance would not cover those other claims.

Although tenants frequently request that the indemnity exclude losses arising from the landlord's negligent or willful act, this does not seem appropriate if the tenant's liability insurance names the landlord as an additional insured or if the indemnity is covered by the contractual liability provision in the tenant's policy. On the other hand, it seems reasonable that if the landlord's negligence or willful act causes a loss that exceeds the amount of liability insurance, the landlord, and not the tenant, should be responsible for the excess over the insurance coverage.

Tenants frequently request that landlords indemnify them against the landlord's acts. Landlords confront several problems in giving indemnities that are as broad as the indemnities that they require from tenants. A landlord should not indemnify a tenant against events that the tenant, but not the landlord, is required to be insured against; a landlord that does agree to such an indemnity could assume liability for which it has no liability insurance coverage. Any landlord's indemnity should carefully exclude liability arising on the premises or for losses caused by the tenant. Essentially, this means that if the landlord is insuring the common areas, the landlord can indemnify the tenant (and obtain contractual liability insurance coverage for such indemnity) for the landlord's acts relative to the common areas.

Goods Owned by Third Parties

Landlords that lease premises to users who store or sell products belonging to third parties, such as public warehouses, third party logistics companies, warehouses used by common carriers, or retail tenants that accept goods on consignment have special problems. The waiver of claims by the tenant does not protect the landlord from liability for damages to goods owned by third parties caused by the landlord's negligence. The value of those goods may well exceed the liability insurance carried by the landlord, especially since the landlord has no way of knowing the value in the first place, so the landlord has no practical way to protect itself. A warehouse operator or the retailer who accepts consignment merchandise can put in its contract a limitation of its liability, but that does not benefit the landlord. The landlord can insist on an indemnity from the tenant (and adequate insurance), but that is expensive and may not be agreeable to the tenant. I can offer no easy solution to this problem, but lawyers for both the landlord and the tenant should be aware of it; not many lawyers are.[7]

Self-Insurance

Many financially strong tenants seek the right to self-insure. This is certainly understandable since the net worth of those companies may exceed that of some insurance carriers, and those tenants may consider the insurance an unnecessary expense. In the alternative, those tenants may seek the right to carry insurance with very large deductibles, and thus insure only catastrophic risks.

Tenants' self-insurance creates risks for landlords. First, what if the strong tenant assigns the lease to a weak one? The right to self-insure should not pass to the assignee. Second, what if the strong tenant suddenly becomes a weak one, as happened so often during the recession, in which once mighty General Motors sought bankruptcy reorganization and a government bail-out? The right should end if the tenant does not maintain a certain tangible net worth.[8] Third, the landlord was counting on the tenant's property insurance to give effect to the waiver of claims and the waiver of the right of subrogation; how does the landlord protect itself against suits for negligent damage to the tenant's property? The lease should specifically provide that the self-insurance is deemed to be insurance for the purpose of those waivers.

---

7. This topic is discussed in greater detail in the article "Allocation of Insurable Risks in Commercial Lease" cited in footnote 1 on page 34.

8. I prefer using "tangible net worth" to plain old "net worth," which might include good will or other intangibles that do not have ready market value.

Summing Up

I have used a lot of space in this book and spent a lot of your time on insurance-related issues. What you have learned here will, I believe, be very useful in your profession. I caution you, however. There is still much I have not covered, and the insurance business, like the real estate business, is not static. What is called Special Form today may well have another name tomorrow, or even by the time you are reading this book. It is a good idea to befriend a good insurance agent whose brain you may pick for information and advice. That is how I learned about insurance. The same advice would apply to any number of experts in other fields that impact leasing.

Assignment and Subletting

First, I would like to clear up a possible misconception. Some people may be under the impression that the difference between a sublease and an assignment is that under an assignment the assignor is released from further obligations under the lease. WRONG! The assignor is not automatically released. That only happens if the assigned lease provides that, or if the landlord agrees at the time to such a release.

So what is the difference between the two?

Under the law, if a tenant transfers all of its interest in the lease and the premises, it is an assignment, no matter what it is called. If the tenant reserves some interest, even if the document is called an assignment, it is actually a sublease. In other words, if the tenant "subleases" the entire premises for the entire term, it is really an assignment. That is why subleases generally end a day or so before the tenant's term ends. Similarly, if the tenant "assigns" the lease but reserves a right of re-entry—the right to take back the space and resume its position as the tenant—if the assignee defaults, that is considered, at law, a sublease. In other words, if there is litigation and it is material whether the document is a sublease or an assignment, those principles will apply. While it is important to keep those principles in the backs of our minds, that is probably where they belong because in practice, most "subleases" are really subleases and most "assignments" are really assignments.

Under an assignment, the tenant parts with all of its rights under the lease (although it remains liable for the non-performance of obligations unless it is expressly released). The assignment creates a direct relationship between the landlord and the assignee as if they had done the lease directly. This is referred to as "privity of contract." While assignments of part of the premises are legally possible, this is almost never done, because of the impracticality of dividing rights and obligations between the assignor and the assignee. Since the assignment is based on the terms and conditions of the existing lease, the assignee is obligated to pay rent at the rate specified in the lease. Hence, assignments are not generally used in situations where the tenant proposes to dispose of the space at a lower rent than it is paying the landlord. There are ways to deal with this, however, as I will discuss below (see page 57).

Although I have discussed the nature of the sublease above (see page 25), there is more to be said about it. Generally, subleases are used when the tenant desires to dispose of all or part of its premises for less than all of its term, or even if it is for all of the term (minus one day), at a rental rate or on other terms different from the original lease. The sublease is, in effect, a new lease between the tenant (as sublandlord) and the subtenant. The privity of contract is not between the subtenant and the landlord (known as the prime landlord, master landlord, or the overlandlord) but between the sublandlord and the subtenant. The subtenant does not have the right to sue the prime landlord if it does not perform its obligations, even if the subtenant is damaged by that. It must have the sublandlord do so, for its benefit, and that should be provided for in the sublease document.

In the assignment situation, if the assignee defaults and the landlord sues the original tenant, that tenant may be able to proceed against the assignee under an indemnity or other agreement in the assignment to perform the obligations under the lease. However, the original tenant does not have the right to kick the assignee out of the space, to resume its position as tenant, and possibly to assign the lease to another assignee or sublease the premises. As I wrote above, if the original tenant reserves a right of re-entry, which it may do, it will be deemed a sublandlord under a sublease, which may have other consequences, such as lack of privity. In the sublease situation, the tenant/sublandlord may in fact evict the subtenant and resume full occupancy of the premises or at least be in a position to sublease it to another subtenant and thus mitigate its damages.

Assignments are often (but not always) used when a tenant is selling its business and is transferring the lease as one of the assets being sold. As I said, subleases are usually used to dispose of unneeded space.

What if your client wishes to assign the lease and get out of the picture completely (perhaps the credit of the assignee is sufficient that the landlord is willing to release your client from future obligations), but the assignee is unwilling to pay the amount of rent specified in the lease? Here is a handy solution to the problem that I have used (and it is also handy in a sub-sublease situation, to avoid over-complication). I provide for the assignor to agree to pay the difference between the lease rent and the rent the assignee is willing to pay. The entire difference may be paid in advance, but at a discounted rate, or it may be paid monthly in advance, or quarterly, or yearly, whatever the parties decide, and the obligation to pay may be secured by a letter of credit from a bank. Although the obligation of the bank under a letter of credit must be secured, by deposit of some assets of the assignor in this case, such letters of credit are not expensive.

Why might a tenant wish to assign its lease or sublease all or a portion of its premises? Most tenants, when they lease space, expect to occupy all of it for the duration of the lease. There are exceptions, of course (as there are to almost every situation described in this book). A tenant may be leasing more space than it needs at the time and intends to sublease the portion it does not need, so it may grow into it; thus it is "warehousing" the extra space. Or a tenant may be in some business where it has a close working relationship with another entity and wants that entity in close proximity.

More commonly, however, the reasons for disposing of the lease or the premises arise from changes in the tenant's business. The tenant may outgrow the space and desire to lease larger premises. A retail tenant may feel that its business would be more successful at a different location. Or the tenant may have suffered a business reversal and wish to downsize or close altogether. And, of course, the tenant may sell its business and have no further need for the space.

Leases generally provide that the landlord's consent is required for a transfer, whether it be by assignment or sublease. If the lease is silent, then the general rule of law is that the tenant's interest in the lease or the premises may be transferred without the landlord's consent (although there may be jurisdictions in which that is not the rule). As you would expect, very few leases are silent on the matter. The real issue is whether the landlord must act reasonably. The law varies from state to state as to whether, if the lease is silent on reasonableness, the landlord must be reasonable. For that reason, it is customary for tenants to insist that the lease provide that the landlord must act reasonably.

What does *reasonable* mean? It is a rather vague standard, but one used in many leases and in connection with many other provisions of leases and contracts. It means that courts (or arbitrators) must decide whether, under all the circumstances, the landlord properly denied the right to transfer.

Many leases have a list of standards as to which a denial or consent will not be deemed unreasonable. Some of the frequently seen standards are:

1. The tenant may not be in default under the lease.
2. The manner of the subtenant's use of the premises after the subletting or assignment, even if consistent with the use clause, may not be detrimental to the property.
3. The proposed subtenant or assignee must be acceptable to the landlord, financially and otherwise.
4. The proposed subtenant or assignee may not be a government agency.
5. The proposed subtenant or assignee may not be a tenant in the building.
6. The proposed subtenant or assignee may not then be negotiating with the landlord for a lease on the property and may not have negotiated with the landlord for space on the property within the prior 12 months.
7. The proposed rental rate in the sublease may not be lower than that quoted by the landlord for comparable space on the property.

Let us consider these standards. As to number 1, why should the tenant not have the right to cure the default (if it is curable) in connection with the transfer? The landlord is made whole and the tenant may proceed to realize its objective in making the transfer. Number 2 goes to the possible change in the way the subtenant plans to operate in premises, which may be detrimental. That seems fair. As to Number 3, how is acceptability to be determined? If the transferee has the financial capacity to perform its obligations, it should not have to be Apple, Inc. And what does *otherwise* mean? Still, this language can be made more specific and the concept survive. What about Number 4? We have already learned about the pros and cons of government leases (see page 24), so we can see why some landlords would not want them in the building. However, this limitation might not be appropriate in Washington, D.C. or a state capital.

Numbers 5, 6, and 7 present real difficulties for tenants. I can understand that a landlord does not want the tenant competing with it for other tenants, but if the space proposed to be transferred is the perfect space for the prospect (who may be the next door neighbor), why should the tenant be prevented from subleasing to it, especially if the landlord does not have other suitable space for that party? How is the tenant supposed to know that the landlord is negotiating with the prospective tenant? And if the negotiations between the landlord and the prospective tenant broke off, what legitimate claim does the landlord have to that prospect? Finally, as to Number 7, most subleases are for a lower rent than the tenant is paying, let alone the rent being quoted for other space on the property, which, except in a down market, is likely to be higher than the tenant's rent; that is essentially a prohibition on subleasing.

Notice that none of the standards above address a change in the permitted use of the premises. That may be because the lease will say that the transferee is bound by all of the provisions of the lease, including the purpose or use clause. The tenant's broker would be wise to protect his or her client's right to transfer the lease for a different use, although the landlord and its broker will be concerned about what a new use might be. In a shopping center situation, for example, the landlord is concerned about tenant mix or possible violations of exclusive rights given to other tenants. A retail landlord might have negotiated a low percentage rent rate (see page 17) suitable for the particular tenant, but the transferee might be selling products that typically generate a higher rate. An industrial/warehouse landlord might be concerned about a use that would risk greater damage to the building, and an office landlord might be concerned about a much higher traffic user.

Another common means by which a landlord seeks to limit its risk of being deemed unreasonable is to limit the tenant's remedies. Ordinarily, if a court holds that a landlord unreasonably withheld consent it could award damages to the tenant for loss of the benefit of the transfer. To be fair to landlords, some decisions are pretty close calls, and a landlord may be induced to consent when it feels it has grounds not to do so, because of the risk of litigation and possible damages. Thus, it is not uncommon to see leases that limit the tenant's remedies to declaratory judgment or injunction. In other words, if the landlord withholds consent, the tenant may sue and ask the court to determine that the landlord was unreasonable (such suits are permitted in most but not all states) or to enjoin the landlord from withholding consent. No damages may be awarded. The problem for the tenant is that any legal proceeding is time-consuming, and by the time the court decides, the prospect will have moved on. With due regard to the landlord's concerns, the remedy proposed is no remedy at all, but it is very difficult to come up with an expedited way to determine reasonableness, and landlords are often simply unwilling to risk a damage award.

There are other ways in which landlords seek to control transfers. You may recall my mentioning some leases made in the 1960s that were 20 years in duration and as to which tenants had the right to assign or sublease pretty freely. Well, from that experience came two new concepts: recapture and sharing of profits.

Recapture means that if a tenant proposes to assign its lease, or sublease the premises or a portion thereof, the landlord may, instead of consenting, terminate the lease or, in the case of a partial sublease, exclude from the premises leased the portion proposed to be subleased. In the exclusion of a portion situation, the space is divided and the rent reduced. In any case, the landlord may lease the premises recaptured to the prospect or hold the premises for leasing to third parties at the market rent at the time. The tenant's obligations are eliminated or reduced, as the case may be, but the landlord and not the tenant makes the profit from leasing the premises. Of course, if the landlord has reasonable grounds for withholding consent, it may elect, instead of exercising its right to terminate, to withhold consent and keep the tenant "on the hook," as we say.

There are certain situations where the tenant has a legitimate objection to a landlord's terminating the lease. For example, if the tenant is proposing to sell its business and is assigning the lease in that connection, a recapture by the landlord might prevent the sale. That exception should be negotiated in the lease at its inception.

Sharing of profits is not, during a downturn in the economy, a major concern, but it might be in inflationary times. Lease forms often provide that if the tenant is making a profit on the transfer, the entire profit goes to the landlord. This is not only unfair, it is foolish. If the tenant gets no portion of the profit, it has no incentive to negotiate a higher rent than it is paying the landlord. Neither party gets anything. A 50/50 split is where the compromise usually comes out. Again, the tenant is worried about how the profit is determined. There are usually expenses involved in finding a new tenant and making changes in the space. Should those expenses come out before the split? What if, as part of an assignment, the tenant is selling equipment, being reimbursed for the unamortized leasehold improvements, being paid for good will as part of the sale of the business, or selling another location? That income is not profit from the transfer of the premises and should be excluded in the lease.

Most leases prohibit the transfer of option rights in connection with an assignment or subletting. Thus, if the lease is assigned two years before its expiration, and the assignee is counting on the right to exercise an existing option in order to continue the business in the premises, it may find, on review of the lease, that option is not transferred with the assignment, and it will have to negotiate an extension with the landlord. I can understand the landlord's position here; an option is a "one-way street" in that the only benefit the landlord gets is that the tenant is willing to sign the lease (which it might not do without the option). Options are discussed further below (see page 78). On the other hand, the tenant may not be able to conclude the sale of the premises or the business because the option is not transferable.

Even if the option is transferable, another issue arises. As I noted above, the tenant remains liable under the lease if it assigns the lease. But what if it assigns the lease and the assignee exercises an option to extend or to take additional premises? Is the tenant liable for the obligations under the lease during the extended term or for the additional premises? I am confident that, in the absence of an agreement in the lease, the answer varies from state to state, but the landlord will certainly want the liability to continue, on the grounds that the exercise of the option was a contingency anticipated in the original lease, and the tenant will certainly want it to end, on the grounds that what the exercise of the option created was, in effect, a new deal. So if any option is transferable, this issue will have to be addressed by the parties, their brokers, and their lawyers.

Many lease forms provide for landlord's consent to a transfer of control of the tenant. The provision may be in substantially the following form:

> If Tenant is an entity, the ownership of which, at the time of execution of this Lease or during the Term, is or shall be held by fewer than 100 persons, and if at any time during the Term the persons, or entities which own a majority of the ownership interests at the time of the execution of this Lease or following Landlord's consent to a transfer of the ownership interests cease to own the majority (except as a result of transfer by bequest or inheritance), and such cessation shall not first have been approved by Landlord, then such cessation shall, at the option of Landlord, be an Event of Default by Tenant.

The rationale for that provision is to prevent the tenant (other than one publicly held) from, in effect, transferring the lease by transferring control of the tenant. The above language is fairer than some I have seen, which does not provide for prior approval by the landlord and may not provide for death transfers. Even this language does not provide for a transfer in connection with estate planning. Still, many tenants object to the concept because it limits the tenant's right to deal with its ownership interest and, in fact, tenants frequently request the right to transfer to a parent, subsidiary, an affiliated entity, or an entity resulting from a merger or consolidation. Landlords usually agree to those transfers, but subject to various conditions, as evidenced by the following:

> Tenant may, without Landlord's consent and without being subject to the provisions of [the section permitting recapture], Transfer this Lease to a parent, an affiliate or a wholly owned subsidiary of Tenant. Any Transfer under this Section shall be conditioned upon (a) Tenant's or such Transferee's having a tangible net worth, after the Transfer, equal to or greater than Tenant's tangible net worth

immediately prior to the Transfer; (b) Tenant is not at that time in default under the Lease; and (c) any guarantor of Tenant's obligations shall agree in writing that the guaranty shall continue in full force and effect, notwithstanding the Transfer. In the event of such a Transfer, Tenant shall give Landlord advance notice thereof and a copy of the Transfer instrument, and shall advise Landlord of the identity of the Transferee and of the identity of the person with whom Landlord may deal in connection with matters relating to the Lease and the Premises.

Tenant may, without Landlord's consent and without being subject to the provisions of [the section permitting recapture], assign this Lease to any entity resulting from a merger or consolidation of Tenant upon the following conditions: (a) the tangible net worth and the total assets of the Transferee after the consolidation or merger shall be equal to or more than that of Tenant immediately prior to the consolidation or merger; (b) Tenant is not at that time in default under the Lease; (c) the successor shall execute an agreement assuming all of the obligations imposed upon Tenant under the Lease and deliver it to Landlord prior to the effective date of the Transfer; and (d) any guarantor of Tenant's obligations shall agree in writing that the guaranty shall continue in full force and effect, notwithstanding the merger or consolidation.

Delivery of Possession, Construction, and Commencement Date

The issues under this heading vary based not only on type of use, but also on the condition of the premises and of the building of which the premises are a part. Thus, the premises may exist in a completed building and are in move-in condition. Under these circumstances, it is customary to say that the premises shall be delivered in "as-is, where-is" condition, although I prefer to say, on behalf of landlords, "in their condition as of the execution and delivery of this lease, reasonable wear and tear excepted." Note that if the landlord is doing any work whatsoever in the premises to prepare them for the tenant's occupancy, even if it is as simple as painting and carpeting, they are not being delivered in "as-is, where-is" condition, and the work to be performed should be described in the lease or in an exhibit attached to the lease (including who is to select the paint color or carpet design).

It is not uncommon for the landlord to have to perform work before delivering possession of the premises to the tenant. That work may involve building a new building, which may be a build-to-suit where the premises are move-in ready, or it may simply be four walls and a roof where the tenant does the final build-out for its own use. More commonly, the landlord's work will be in an existing building and may range from checking and repairing the mechanical systems, or cleaning out debris or equipment left by the prior tenant, to construction to prepare existing premises for the new tenant's use, or at least for that tenant's own construction. In an industrial/warehouse building, the landlord's work might consist of constructing some office space or even demolishing the prior tenant's office space. The landlord might be running additional power to the premises, constructing a demising wall to separate the premises from other space, or erecting interior walls and running power or heated and chilled water to a single location, leaving it to the tenant to do the finishing work in the space, distribute the power, and convert heated and chilled water to actual heating and air conditioning. In the latter situation, the landlord is commonly said to deliver a "vanilla box" to the tenant. The tenant's obligation to complete the space is usually described in considerable detail in the lease or, more commonly, in a work letter agreement attached as an exhibit to the lease. The possibilities are nearly endless.

Retail users often have very specific requirements for the conduct of their business and desire to do the build out of their space themselves. Chain retailers may have a template design and use the same architects and designers all over the country. They are happy to receive a vanilla box so that they may build the space to their specifications. Retailers, generally, may be very specific about what the landlord is constructing, as well as the timing of the work, since, for example, they may want to be open in time for the Christmas season.

Of course, the deal may call for the landlord to build out the space to the tenant's specifications in what is referred to as a "turn-key" build-out.

Leases and work letter agreements tend to be pretty specific about the landlord's required work, and since they are generally drafted for landlords, they tend to be even more specific about the tenant's work. However, they are often subject to considerable negotiation. What happens if the landlord is delayed in the performance of its work? What if the delay is caused by the tenant? What constitutes completion or, more commonly, substantial completion of the landlord's work? How are disputes about whether the work is substantially completed to be resolved?

The landlord is, obviously, concerned about what will be built by the tenant in its building. It wants to see and approve plans and specifications, it wants to make certain that all legal requirements are met, and it wants to ensure that required permits and certificates of occupancy are obtained by the tenant. It is concerned that the contractors working in the building are reputable and qualified to perform the work and that they will not damage the building or interfere with other tenants. The documents may require that the contractor employ union labor, particularly if the landlord uses union labor. The landlord wants to make certain that no mechanic's liens are filed against the building or, if they are filed, that the liens be contested promptly and properly and that the property is secured against an adverse decision in the contest. The landlord also wants to ensure that the work is completed on schedule so that the tenant may begin paying rent on time.

Who pays for the work is a critical economic issue. Typically, the landlord pays for the landlord's work. If the landlord is performing the work on a "turn-key" basis, the lease may cap the landlord's cost exposure, with the tenant required to pay any difference, either in the form of a rent increase or in cash (sometimes over time with an interest factor built in). When the tenant is performing the work, it may negotiate a construction allowance covering all or a portion of the cost of that work. Of course, the landlord is not paying a construction allowance out of the goodness of its heart (if it has one). The cost of the construction allowance (as well as other construction by the landlord) is factored in to the rent payable by the tenant.[9] The lease may specify that the construction allowance may be used only for actual hard and soft construction costs, and not for furniture, fixtures, and equipment (FF&E), because the landlord wants its money to go into the building.[10] The lease may also specify that excess construction allowance may not be applied as a rent credit, although in my judgment, that is unfair since the cost of the construction allowance is factored into the rent, and if the landlord does not fund the entire construction allowance and does not reduce the rent, it is getting the money twice.

So when does the lease commence? That is not such an easy question, either, since the lease may commence at different times for different purposes. Obviously, when the landlord delivers possession of the premises to the tenant, the lease starts for some purposes. The tenant is entitled to the possession to perform its work. It must, during that time, carry insurance, possibly pay for utilities, and perform other obligations. But has the "term" commenced? The "term" is defined as the period of years specified in the lease between what is usually referred to as the "commencement date" and the end of the lease. Often, the term *"commencement date"* is the earlier of (1) the date the tenant opens for business in the premises and (2) the date for commencement specified in the lease (which may be a set number of days after landlord delivers the premises with landlord's work substantially completed).

Does the rent start on the term commencement date? Maybe yes, and maybe no. If the tenant has negotiated a rent concession, such as six months free rent, the rent commencement date will be later than the term commencement date, and certainly later than the delivery date. On the other hand, it is possible, although unusual, that the parties may provide that the rent will commence on the delivery date, or some other date—it is all a matter of the agreement of the parties.

Let me add a word about "as-built" plans, which are often required by the landlord after tenant's work (or any alteration) is completed. There are

---

9. Who pays the cost of construction has tax effects, as well, since the right to depreciate them has value.

10. Hard costs are the actual costs of physical construction; soft costs are architectural and engineering fees, permits, and similar necessary related costs.

two types of "as-built" plans. One is the set of working drawings marked as construction plans to indicate construction changes from the original plans. If, for example, an electrical outlet cannot be located where shown on the working drawings, the actual location will be shown on the marked working drawings. The other "as-built" plans are those prepared by architects after the project has been completed. This is a time-consuming and expensive project and is generally not really needed by the landlord, who just wants to know what the premises look like after the work and does not need an expensive and fancy drawing. In any case, the lease should state which type of "as-built" plans are required.

Alterations

Alterations provisions present many of the same issues as initial leasehold improvements. The landlord wants to know and approve of what is being performed in the premises; it wants to know that the alterations are legal; it wants to approve the contractor; it wants to make certain that the tenant can pay for the alterations and that it will be protected from possible lien claims. But there are additional issues to be considered in connection with proposed alterations.

The landlord may want the right to perform the alterations itself, at the tenant's cost, using the landlord's own contractor. Certainly, if there is to be roof work, the landlord wants to make sure that there is no violation of any roof warranty, and the best way to ensure that is to have the landlord's roofing contractor perform the work. The landlord may have a legitimate concern that the tenant will contract with unqualified but inexpensive contractors (or use the tenant's own employees).

On the other hand, the tenant is concerned about the cost of the work and can foresee that it will cost it more money if the landlord does the alteration. If the landlord allows the tenant to perform the work with its own contractors or employees, the landlord may still want the right to monitor the work (for which it will certainly insist on receiving a fee). In any case, the tenant will want the right to perform redecorating or minor work without the hassle of the full-blown requirements typical in alterations sections. The parties will have to negotiate just what constitutes minor work, probably based on the cost of the work (with a limited yearly aggregate).

Another issue is what is to happen to the alterations at the end of the term. Usually the "surrender" provision of the lease (see page 112) deals with removal of alterations, but it seems to me that the alterations section is the proper place to deal with that issue. The tenant should request that the lease require the landlord to decide, when it consents to the alteration, whether the alterations must be removed by the tenant upon surrender. Sometimes landlords are willing to agree to that, but sometimes they feel that they cannot make the decision at that time because the value of the alteration at the end of the term will depend on whether it might be useful or detrimental to a succeeding tenant. If the landlord is willing to decide the issue when requested to approve the alteration, however, it is my view that the tenant should be required to ask for such a decision as part of its request for the approval of the alteration. After all, the landlord may forget that it must decide at that time, leaving the matter in a sort of limbo.

In addition, it is in the tenant's interest to have the landlord decide not only whether it will require removal but also whether, instead, it will require that the alteration be left in place. The alteration may be useful to the tenant after removal, and the tenant may want to know whether it can take the alteration with it. Needless to say, the landlord will require that the tenant repair any damage caused by the removal and perhaps even that the tenant restore the premises to their condition prior to the making of the alteration.

Mechanic's Liens

Just about every state has mechanic's lien laws to protect the rights of contractors to be paid for construction. The problem is that the lien laws vary greatly from state to state. Any construction done on premises, whether it be initial leasehold improvements performed in accordance with a workletter agreement or alterations, may create a right of the contractor (or its subcontractors or material suppliers) to file a lien claim, the effect of which is to encumber the property and, if the lien is held to be valid and the claim remains unpaid, to result in a foreclosure sale of the property. You can easily see that this would be very damaging to the landlord, the other tenants, and even to the tenant causing the lien. For that reason, leases tend to be very strict about preventing lien claims and, if any are filed, to require that they be satisfied right away.

However (and there seems always to be a "however" in this book), the lien claim may not be legitimate. The work may not have been done, or done satisfactorily. The contractor may, in fact, have already been paid, but may claim payment for extras that were not authorized. The lien claim may have been filed too late or be defective for some other reason. There can be any number of defenses to the claim, and the tenant typically asks for a right to contest the lien claim and not to be considered in default until the contest is resolved. In many states, the tenant would have the right to bond over the lien claim in court, so the lien claim is, from a title examination standpoint, discharged. In Illinois, where I practice, that procedure is not available, so we typically require the tenant to cause a title insurance company to insure over the lien claim (the title company would require an indemnity and a deposit of security to do so) or that the tenant deposit security with the landlord to ensure that the claim, and all interest and costs, will be paid if the tenant loses the contest.

Maintenance

As I discussed above, triple net leases in single-tenant buildings frequently require the tenant to perform all maintenance (except for those items specifically reserved as the landlord's responsibility) (see page 12). I discussed those triple-net leases in terms of industrial/warehouse leasing, but single-tenant office or retail leases may also be triple-net where the tenant performs all maintenance. In all those situations, it is typical for maintenance to include replacement of items or features that can no longer be repaired. It is important for the landlord to specify what items of replacement are the tenant's responsibility or are charged to the tenant, because in the absence of such specificity, a court might rule that since replacements are typically a landlord function, the landlord will have to pay for them.

If the landlord has agreed to maintain roof and structure, both parties should understand the precise scope of the landlord's responsibility so that a clear line can be drawn between the duties of each of them. If the tenant is to repair the roof until it can no longer be repaired, how and when is it determined that the landlord must replace it? Does the "roof" include the structural portions that underlie the roof membrane? What about flashings and other components of the roof? As to structure, is the landlord's responsibility limited to conditions that arise due to defects in the original construction, or does it include conditions resulting from deterioration? Who is responsible for tuck pointing? What if the tenant's negligence or the nature of its use causes the problem? All of these questions must be answered in the lease and thus considered in the negotiation of the lease. It is obvious that the answers to the questions will have substantial economic impact on the parties.

Getting beyond roof and structure, a very contentious issue is the condition of HVAC equipment, particularly roof-top units. Usually, the tenant will ask for the landlord to at least put that equipment in working condition before the lease commences. Beyond that, the tenant may agree to perform maintenance but seek to have the landlord replace the equipment if that becomes necessary during the term. Those issues can lead to a lot of discussion about payment for the cost of replacement and with the tenant arguing that the new equipment will have a useful life after the lease is over, so the landlord should pay the entire cost—and the landlord arguing that the tenant has the benefit of the useful life of the existing equipment, so the tenant should pay the entire cost. Both arguments have some validity, so the parties usually reach some compromise about sharing the cost.

In a multi-tenant building leased on a net basis where the landlord advances the costs of certain maintenance but the tenants reimburse the landlord for their share of those costs, the issues are essentially the same. In gross leases with stops, the landlord's maintenance obligations are spelled out, and the cost of the landlord's performance is usually covered in operating expenses or common area expenses. Here again, the parties will discuss what portion of the cost of repair or replacement of certain items should be charged to the tenant, and the parties may agree to amortize so-called "capital" costs over the useful life of the item, with some interest factor, and with the tenant paying amortization only during the term of its lease (and any extensions).

Most leases provide that the tenant is obligated to maintain the interior of its premises (and, in the case of single-tenant buildings, the exterior, as well). Disputes may arise as to underground pipes, and they are usually resolved by specifying that tenant is responsible only for those that serve its premises. Most leases also provide that, unless the repair or replacement is to be paid for out of insurance proceeds, the tenant must repair, replace, or pay for items that it or its contractors, suppliers, employees, or customers damage—even if those items were otherwise the responsibility of the landlord.

It is not unusual for the lease to require the tenant to arrange for a maintenance contract for certain equipment. HVAC equipment, for example, will have a much shorter life if it is not inspected and serviced regularly. The same applies to elevators and escalators, as failure to maintain them may cost the landlord a lot of money after the lease is over.

Damage or Destruction

If a fire or other casualty occurs, the parties will rush to view the lease to determine their rights and obligations; that may be the only time after execution that the lease is ever taken out of the drawer. Except in a single-tenant lease where the tenant has undertaken repair and restoration, the obligation to restore will be the landlord's. There will usually be a time period before the landlord is obligated to commence the restoration and either an obligation to proceed with due diligence or to complete the restoration within a specified period of time. The lease will usually provide that the rent will abate while, and to the extent that, the premises are not useable by the tenant for the operation of its business.

Some leases provide that the landlord will restore the base building and that the tenant is obligated to restore the balance. This might mean that the landlord will again deliver a vanilla box to the tenant and the tenant has to rebuild its leasehold improvements, or it might mean that the landlord will restore to the condition prior to the performance of alterations by the tenant, but that the tenant has to restore its own alterations. Usually, this is tied in with the tenant's obligation to carry insurance on its improvements. In my view, these requirements are inappropriate for the reasons stated above (see page 42). Typically, mortgages require the landlord to insure the building and to have the insurance proceeds payable to the lender so that the lender may apply them to pay down the loan or to the restoration of the property (see page 43). It is in the landlord's interest that it control all of the restoration and not have numerous different contractors swarming around the building at the same time. From the tenant's standpoint, it may have had to do build-out once, but that is not what it is in business to do.

As to the rent abatement, leases often provide that the rent commences again when the landlord completes its restoration work. This should certainly not be the case if the tenant has to restore its improvements or alterations, and it should not be the case, as well, if the tenant has to re-fixture the premises and install its equipment, merchandise, and other personal property. The tenant should be afforded a reasonable period of time to do so.

Leases sometimes give the landlord the right to terminate the lease if certain conditions exist, such as the length of time that will be required to restore, or the fact that all or substantially all of the (multi-tenant) building has been destroyed. They do not usually give the tenant the same right, except possibly close to the end of the term or if the restoration is not commenced when required in the lease, or completed within some period—which the landlord will want to be an extended period. The landlord has a good reason for that: If the tenant has the right to terminate, the lender may not make the insurance proceeds available to restore and the landlord will have to refinance the property in order to do so (assuming the loan is pre-payable). New financing may not be readily available (it will be a construction loan) or the rate may be substantially higher than the rate with the existing lender (which may be why the lender is so eager to retain the proceeds).

Sometimes a lease form will provide that the landlord's right to terminate is triggered by the premises being untenantable, which means that they may not be occupied. This is really unfair to the tenant since the premises may be untenantable for reasons other than material damage to the premises themselves. For example, there may be water damage in the premises because of a fire on an upper floor or the elevators are unusable due to a fire and the tenant cannot access its upper-level space. In that case, the landlord may terminate the lease because it wants to get more rent in an up-market, not because of the damage. If untenantability is the standard, it should be tied to some substantial duration. A better standard for termination is that it would take a long specified time to restore, or that the cost of restoration exceeds a specified number. If the landlord terminates and then restores the premises, perhaps the tenant should be afforded a right to lease the space again on the same terms as before; that right will keep the landlord honest.

I have already discussed the inadvisability of conditioning the rent abatement on the tenant's not having caused the fire (see page 45). Such a provision is not in the interest of any party except the insurance company, which does not then have to pay the proceeds of the rent insurance that was paid for, directly or indirectly, by the tenant.

Subordination and Non-Disturbance

We are dealing here with the question: Which has priority, the lease or the mortgage? If a mortgage is executed, delivered, and recorded before a lease is executed and delivered, the lender has priority over the lease, and if it forecloses, it can wipe the lease out.[11] If the lease is executed and delivered before the mortgage, and the mortgagee has notice (by recording of a memorandum of lease) or actual knowledge of the existence of the lease (such as by inspecting the property and seeing the tenant building out the space or conducting its business), the lease has priority, and if there is a foreclosure, the lender cannot wipe out the lease. So far, so good?

What happens if your tenant client is about to sign a lease where it will be spending a lot of money to fix the place up, or the lease is for a long term and/or for a lot of space, and there is already a mortgage in place? How do you protect your tenant? You make certain that the tenant gets a Non-Disturbance Agreement, that's how! "What is a Non-Disturbance

---

11. Recording is not generally a condition if the tenant has actual knowledge of the existence of the mortgage, but mortgages are almost universally recorded.

Agreement?" you ask. It is an agreement by the lender with the priority position that, if there is a foreclosure, neither it, nor another party that buys at the foreclosure sale, will evict that tenant.[12]

A simple agreement not to evict—the "non-disturbance" aspect of the agreement—is fine, but it certainly does not go far enough. The tenant must also be concerned about who will perform the obligations of the landlord under the lease after the foreclosure. Who will arrange to have the offices cleaned, maintain the roof and structure, or remove snow and ice from the parking lot if those undertakings by the landlord are included in the lease? The tenant needs an undertaking in the agreement by the lender to do those things. It is sometimes referred to in the agreement as "recognition," or there is simply an agreement to perform the obligations.

That agreement is not open-ended, however. A lender will, typically, not agree to return a security deposit if it has not actually received it from the landlord; it will not agree to cure landlord defaults that occurred before the lender took over the property (except, possibly, a continuing default); it will not agree be bound by payments of rent more than one month in advance (if the rent is payable monthly); and it will not agree to be bound by tenant's right to set off any amounts due to the tenant because of a default by the original landlord against future payments of rent. The lender will also require that the tenant "attorn" to the lender if the lender becomes the successor landlord by reason of the foreclosure. *Attorn* simply means that the tenant becomes bound to perform its obligations for the benefit of the lender, just as the lender has agreed to become bound to perform obligations for the tenant's benefit.

The provisions of a Non-Disturbance Agreement may be negotiable to some extent. For example, if the landlord has agreed to a tenant allowance, the lender may agree to allow the tenant to set off any unpaid allowance against rent payable after the foreclosure. This is extremely important in leases where a tenant is to receive a substantial payment to help pay for

---

12. The same principle applies if the landlord is actually a tenant under a ground lease. If the ground lease exists prior to your tenant's lease, that ground lessor would have the right to terminate the ground lease if its lessee (your landlord) defaults, which would, in the absence of a non-disturbance agreement, cause the eviction of the tenant.

tenant improvements. Otherwise, the payment right might be lost in the foreclosure.

Sometimes the lease itself provides that the tenant will not be disturbed and will be entitled to recognition in the event of a foreclosure. That provision is useless to the tenant. The agreement must come from the lender who then has a mortgage on the property. The agreement should also be recorded in order to protect the tenant if the mortgage is assigned by the lender or if someone other than the lender buys the property at the foreclosure sale (or subsequently from the lender itself). If a Non-Disturbance Agreement cannot be signed simultaneously with the execution of the lease, then a tenant who needs the protection should reserve the right to terminate the lease if the agreement is not concluded within a specified period. Before agreeing to that, the landlord should contact its mortgagee to make certain that it will be able to obtain the Non-Disturbance Agreement.

If the lease has priority over a new mortgage, the lender might ask the tenant to subordinate its prior position to the lender. Many lease forms provide that the tenant will subordinate its positions to a new mortgagee but do not condition the tenant's obligation to do so on the mortgagee's agreeing to recognition and non-disturbance. That is unfair to the tenant; why should the tenant be required to give up a right it already has by being first-in-time without adequate protection? In my judgment, even small tenants should negotiate that protection. That is the fair result. The lease should be revised to provide that if the lender requires subordination, it will be obligated to provide non-disturbance and recognition, as described above, as part of the subordination agreement.

My discussion of subordination and non-disturbance highlights a basic principle in lease review, which cannot be emphasized enough: ***Every provision in a lease has an economic effect.*** It is there to provide some benefit, protection, cost, or risk to the parties. Every provision, even the most mundane or obscure, must be carefully considered. ***There are no "boiler plate" provisions in a lease.***

Condemnation

Properties are sometimes taken for some public or quasi-public purpose by a governmental agency or other entity (sometimes even a utility) having the power of eminent domain. For example, a property, or part of a property, may be taken for a road widening, an airport expansion, to build a school, or for public transportation purposes. A municipality may want to change the grade of a street and the result is to render the adjoining property unusable for its existing purpose. These are all "takings" or "condemnations" and the condemning body is obligated under the United States Constitution to pay "just compensation," commonly known as the "award."

Every lease has a section dealing with condemnation that usually favors the landlord, and the parties sometimes spend endless hours negotiating that section. Often, that is a waste of time. Why? Because the likelihood of a taking in any given situation is remote. Sometimes the parties may be surprised and be subject to an unexpected condemnation, but to be realistic, a high-rise building in the central business district of a major city is not going to be condemned.

Consider a total taking, when the lease is terminated. In a ground lease situation, if the landlord owns the land and the tenant owns the building, at least during the term of the lease, each party has a measurable loss from the taking and can legitimately argue for a substantial portion of the condemnation award. In a long-term lease for a big box store, the tenant has some argument to share in the award, since it is losing the benefit of its bargain—and it may also have the economic clout to get something. In the more typical lease, however, the landlord is losing its property and its lender is entitled to have its loan paid off.

Although the tenant is certainly losing its leasehold estate (which is an interest in the property), and it is losing the benefit of its lease, which may be a rental rate below current market or a very favorable location, it is not likely to be able to convince the landlord or its lender to share the award with it. The tenant may get moving expenses or the cost of any personal property taken (although it can probably remove and keep that property) as part of a separate award, or it may be able to squeeze out something for the unamortized value of expensive leasehold improvements or alterations (unlikely), but generally it will need a lot of bargaining clout to get much of a share of the landlord's award.

In the case of a taking of a part of the property, leases sometime tie termination of the lease to the percentage of the premises taken. That is inappropriate because the location of the portion of the premises taken, not the size of the taking, will probably dictate whether the space still has value to the tenant for the conduct of its business. A better standard is whether the premises can still be used for the same purpose and with substantially the same utility to the tenant as before the taking. In either case, if the lease is not terminated, the landlord will customarily agree to restore the balance of the premises (but not to spend more than the award) and to reduce the rent on some equitable basis.

Options and Other Special Rights of Tenants

Let's turn to something with a bit more pizzazz than casualty losses and condemnation. While not usually in the landlord's lease form, options, rights of first refusal, and rights of first offer are often conditions to making a deal. There may be an option to extend the term (I prefer to refer to *extension* rather than to *renewal* because *renewal* may be construed to include further rights to extend), or to lease additional premises, or even to purchase the property.[13] The tenant might insist on a right of first refusal to lease the adjoining space or to buy the building if the landlord decides to sell. The parties might agree that the landlord will offer to lease adjoining space or even to sell the building to the tenant before going to the market, which is commonly known as a right of first offer.

As I said before (see page 61), options are "one-way streets." So are rights of first refusal and rights of first offer. Why is this so? It is because the landlord is restricted in its ability to deal with its property, but the tenant is not bound in any way other than to observe the terms of the right—and then

---

13. There may be rights to terminate the lease or exclude portions of the premises. They are also options but not customarily referred to as such.

only if it desires to exercise the right. For example, assume the tenant has an option to extend the term, and the tenant really wants to continue its lease. It will make a determination whether the rent during the extension that is specified in the lease is a fair rental under the then existing market conditions (a broker representing tenants in the same geographic area may be consulted for the information). If the specified rent is lower than the market, the tenant will exercise the option. If it is higher, the tenant will not exercise the option but will attempt to negotiate an extension at the then current market rate. Of course, the landlord may not really want to keep this tenant, either because it has not been a great tenant or because another tenant (who may be larger or have better credit) needs the space. In that case, the tenant may have to exercise the option, even at a higher-than-market rent, in order to stay in the space. In either case, it is the tenant rather than the landlord that benefits. Similar logic applies to the other rights covered by this section of the book.

I have listed three rights at the beginning of this section: options, rights of first refusal, and rights of first offer. What are the differences?

Options

If the tenant has an option, it has been afforded a continuing irrevocable offer, either to extend the term, take additional space, buy the building, or whatever else was provided in the option language, in accordance with the pre-designated terms specified in the lease. Even if the rent for the extended term is to be determined by some form of appraisal, the way the appraisal is to be conducted is (or should be) set forth in the option provision in the lease. All that the tenant needs to do to accept the continuing offer is to exercise the option in the manner and within the time period specified in the option language.

An example might help. Assume that the tenant has an option to lease the adjoining space in an office building. In well-drafted language, the suite number and size of the space will be set out (and perhaps even a drawing, to show the dimensions). The rent to be paid, any rent concessions, landlord construction, or tenant allowance will also be specified. If the space is to be leased on a gross lease basis with stops, the new base will be specified, if appropriate. The other terms of the original lease will be reviewed by the drafter and his or her counterpart to determine whether all the other terms of the original lease apply, or whether there is a need to include other provisions relating specifically to the option space. If the rent is to be based on "market," the relevant market will be defined (by geographic area and by quality of building), the decision-maker or makers (whether appraisers or brokers—I prefer brokers because they know the terms of deals in the relevant market), and the method of deciding will be included. A fuller discussion of market rent starts on page 116.

The method I like is for each party to choose a broker, who is not related to either party. Each broker comes up with a rent. If the rent determined by the higher is within 10% of the lower, the designated rent is averaged. If the 10% formula does not work, the brokers select a third broker who makes the decision. There are, however, other good methods for resolution of disagreements between each party's broker. In any case, because the various methods for determining "market" rent are expensive and time-consuming, and because the amount of the rent is not the only factor to be considered in determining "market," the parties do not usually resort to any agreed-to method, but manage somehow to agree on the terms.

In the case of a market rent deal, the tenant might seek to have the right to revoke its exercise of the option if it is not satisfied with the rent, or there may be a way for the rent to be determined before the exercise of the option. That makes it even more of a "one-way street." However, if the landlord reserves the right to terminate the option if it is not satisfied with the rent, it is not much of an option since the landlord has, in effect, the right to revoke the continuing offer described above.

Options specify a time period within which they must be exercised, or the occurrence of an event that triggers the option. An option to extend may have to be exercised six months or more before the end of the term. The length of time is often heavily negotiated since the tenant wants to have as short a period as possible so it can evaluate its business and needs based on conditions the tenant anticipates will exist in the future. The landlord, however, wants a long period so it has time to lease the option space (or sell the building) before the tenant's lease expires. Of course, larger spaces, or spaces with specialized uses, take longer to lease, and the landlord will want even longer periods in those situations.

If the rent or price is to be market-determined, the parties will usually agree that the option cannot be exercised before a certain date so that the consideration will actually reflect the then current market conditions. Generally speaking, the option must be exercised with the time specified, or the exercise is not effective. For that reason, it is important that the parties review the notice section of the lease to determine whether notices are effective when sent or when received, since a notice may be sent before the time to exercise expires but received after (remember that I mentioned that even notice provisions have economic effect). Many leases provide that "time is of the essence" and in some jurisdictions, unless that language is included, courts will be lenient if the exercise date is missed and the right is exercised somewhat late. In other jurisdictions, that is not an issue. The right must be exercised on time.

Rights of First Refusal

If a tenant has a right of first refusal, such as to lease adjoining space, the landlord may offer to lease that space to the tenant, and if they are able to reach agreement, the right of first refusal does not take effect. However, if the landlord and the tenant cannot agree on the terms, or if the landlord does not want to lease the premises in question to this tenant, the landlord may go to the market and negotiate a lease for the space with another party. If the landlord finds that third party, it must negotiate the terms of the lease relative to that space—whether a letter of intent will do or the parties must actually negotiate the lease is a matter to be handled in the drafting. When the terms are agreed upon, however, the landlord must then go to the tenant, disclose the terms of the other deal, and then the tenant has some period of time, usually a short period because the other party will not wait forever, to lease the space on the same terms and conditions. The same procedure applies in the case of a right of first refusal to buy or even to lease the same space at the expiration of the term. What happens if the landlord is unable to find the "other party" before the lease expires will have to be dealt with in the negotiations.

It sounds like a good idea; after all, what could be a fairer test of value and of market terms than what a third party is willing to agree to?

Actually, I despise rights of first refusal and will bend every effort to prevent my client from agreeing to them. Why?

1. It is unfair to the third party. If the third party knew in advance that it was being used to determine value and might not get the deal it bargained for, it would not be willing to spend the time, and more importantly the money, to negotiate the deal (particularly if it had to finalize the document before the "offer" was submitted to the tenant). Of course, the landlord could tell the third party about the right of first refusal and hope that the third party wants the space so badly that it is willing to take the risk, but the chances are that the third party would simply walk away. Wouldn't you advise your client to do so?

2. It is unfair to the landlord. The landlord, too, has to go through the time and expense of negotiating the other deal. Certainly, the effort will not be wasted because one or the other party will be bound, but still, the landlord has the unpleasant choice of telling the third party that there is a right of first refusal and possibly watching the third party disappear, or fail to disclose and be in what is certainly an unethical position. If the landlord uses a broker to market the space to third parties, then the broker is the party confronted with the dilemma of disclosing or not disclosing, plus a further dilemma of having to follow the landlord's decision not to disclose or walking away from the deal. The landlord has another issue. It may have agreed with the tenant's broker to pay a full commission on the expansion, purchase, or whatever was the subject matter of the right of first refusal, and the broker representing the third party may claim a commission, even if the right is exercised, on the ground that he or she was actually the procuring cause of the exercise of the right, by bringing to the table the third party who was ready, willing, and able to do the deal.

3. It is not such a great thing for tenants, either. The main problem is that the time for the tenant to exercise the right is usually pretty short—five to seven days at most. That is because the landlord cannot expect the third party to wait around, whether it knows about the right or not. This puts a lot of pressure on the tenant to make a decision very quickly and that is hard to accomplish, particularly in big companies.

The more the tenant presses for a longer time to decide, the more unfair the right becomes for the landlord and the third party.

Needless to say, even when all the problems with rights of first refusal are described, parties still insist on them, particularly tenants. Still, there is an alternative that I suggest, that will satisfy the tenant, and that is the right of first offer.

Rights of First Offer

In granting a right of first offer, the landlord agrees that, before going to market to lease the adjoining space, or sell the building, or whatever is the subject matter of the right, it will offer it to the tenant. That offer will set forth the consideration to be paid by the tenant, which the landlord agrees will be based on a good faith estimate of the true value, and the tenant will have a period of time, usually longer than under the right of first refusal, to accept the landlord's offer. And it may afford the parties an opportunity to negotiate a deal after the offer is made to the tenant without the pressure of a third party offer.

Assume, however, that the following negotiation occurs in connection with a right of first offer to lease the adjoining space. "Okay," says the tenant, "but what if the rent you quoted is not really the market rent and you and I cannot negotiate an acceptable rent? I trust you, but what if you sell the building and your successor is not so honorable?" (The hypothetical evil successor is a very handy foil in lease negotiations.)

This is a very legitimate concern with rights of first offer, so here is a proposed solution.

Right of First Offer with a Back-End Right of First Refusal

This approach combines the right of first offer with a means to determine value if the parties are unable to agree. It works like this: The landlord specifies a price or rent, as the case may be, and the tenant may accept that amount or make a counteroffer. If the tenant makes a counteroffer, the parties have a certain length of time to agree, but if they are unable to do so, the landlord goes to the market and gets an offer from a disinterested third party, just as in the case of the right of first refusal. Then, if the landlord is willing to accept an offer or to make an offer to a third party for a price or rent that is less than the greater of (i) 95% (or another specified percentage) of the offer price or rent specified by the landlord and (ii) the counteroffer price or rent offered by the tenant, the tenant has the right to lease or purchase the property at the price offered by the third party that was acceptable to the landlord.

That is a bit complicated, so an example might be helpful. Assume that the right of first offer relates to the purchase of the property of which the premises are a part. Let's say that the landlord makes a "first offer" to sell the property to the tenant for $10 million. The tenant's highest counteroffer is $9.3 million and the parties cannot agree. The landlord goes to the market and gets a $9.5 million offer from a third party that the landlord desires to accept. The landlord can then sell the property to the third party; the price is 95% of the landlord's offer. If the third party offer is $9.49 million, however, the tenant has the right to match that offer and buy the property because the price is less than 95% of the landlord's offer. If the tenant's offer was $9.6 million, and the third party offer that the landlord desired to accept is $9.55 million, that was less than the tenant's counteroffer, and the landlord would be obligated to re-offer the property to the tenant for $9.55 million. Complicated? Sure!

The point is not necessarily that the parties will use these formulas to determine the price or the rent. The point is that, because the parties will be concerned about the outcome and the cost and delay of getting to that outcome, they will communicate even before the first offer is made by the landlord and agree on a price or rent, or a simple formula for determining it. The parties may fight over the language in the lease, but if the contemplated situation arises, the parties will probably figure out a way to resolve the issues without following the procedures fought over.

Accessibility

The Americans With Disabilities Act of 1990 and regulations and guidelines promulgated under it, as they may be amended and supplemented from time to time (the ADA), is federal law pertaining to accessibility for persons with disabilities.

Title III of the ADA establishes requirements pertaining to business operations, accessibility, and barrier removal. Those requirements may be unclear, and may or may not apply to the various premises, buildings, or the properties depending on, among other things: (a) whether the tenant's business operations are deemed a "place of public accommodation" or a "commercial facility," (b) whether compliance with such requirements is "readily achievable" or "technically infeasible," and (c) whether a given condition or alteration affects a "primary function area" or triggers so-called "path of travel" requirements.

The ADA has a specific list of what is deemed a place of public accommodation, as follows:

(A) an inn, hotel, motel, or other place of lodging, except for an establishment located within a building that contains not more than five rooms for rent or hire and that is actually occupied by the proprietor of such establishment as the residence of such proprietor;

(B) a restaurant, bar, or other establishment serving food or drink;

(C) a motion picture house, theater, concert hall, stadium, or other place of exhibition or entertainment;

(D) an auditorium, convention center, lecture hall, or other place of public gathering;

(E) a bakery, grocery store, clothing store, hardware store, shopping center, or other sales or rental establishment;

(F) a laundromat, dry-cleaner, bank, barber shop, beauty shop, travel service, shoe repair service, funeral parlor, gas station, office of an accountant or lawyer, pharmacy, insurance office, professional office of a health care provider, hospital, or other service establishment;

(G) a terminal, depot, or other station used for specified public transportation;

(H) a museum, library, gallery, or other place of public display or collection;

(I) a park, zoo, amusement park, or other place of recreation;

(J) a nursery, elementary, secondary, undergraduate, or postgraduate private school, or other place of education;

(K) a day care center, senior citizen center, homeless shelter, food bank, adoption agency, or other social service center establishment; and

(L) a gymnasium, health spa, bowling alley, golf course, or other place of exercise or recreation.

Other businesses, such as warehouses or offices not listed above, are categorized as "commercial facilities." Under the ADA, the standard for accessibility for places of public accommodation is much greater than for commercial facilities. This is a highly technical area of the law and it is not appropriate to delve into it too much here, but real estate lawyers should be aware of the issues and, if appropriate, seek counsel from lawyers or architects with expertise in this area. They should also be aware that many states and local governments have accessibility requirements that may or may not exceed the national standard.

The main accessibility issue for lawyers is the allocation of responsibility for compliance. This is, of course, a matter of negotiation based on market conditions and the respective situations of the parties.

Covenant of Quiet Enjoyment

The covenant of quiet enjoyment certainly has nothing to do with noise. It has to do with title.

The law implies a covenant of quiet enjoyment in every lease—an agreement by the landlord that the tenant's use and occupancy of the premises will not be disturbed by other claimants. In other words, if the landlord did not really own the property when it signed the lease and put the tenant in possession of the premises, and the tenant is evicted by the real owner or the real owner demands an exorbitant increase in rent, that constitutes a breach of the covenant, which gives rise to a cause of action by the tenant against the landlord. Likewise, if the landlord mortgages the premises and, as a result of a foreclosure, the tenant is evicted, the tenant could seek damages from the landlord.

Most leases contain a "Covenant of Quiet Enjoyment" section, but if you review it, you will find that it is not very broad. In fact, it is less broad than the implied covenant. For example, the section might read:

> So long as no Event of Default by Tenant has occurred, Tenant's quiet and peaceable enjoyment of the premises shall not be disturbed or interfered with by Landlord or by any person claiming by, through or under Landlord.

As you can see, this language does nothing to protect the tenant against a claimant with a prior right to the premises.

The covenant of quiet enjoyment, while it is in every lease and is somewhat interesting to consider, no longer has the same impact as it used to have. In most commercial leases these days, the landlord is an entity that owns nothing other than the property, all or a portion of which is leased to the tenant. It is a corporation or a limited liability company or even a trust, and probably is a single-purpose entity. If the tenancy is interfered with by a prior claimant or by the landlord's lender and as a result, the landlord loses the property, recourse against the landlord is useless since the particular landlord has nothing left. The tenant does not have any right of recourse against the owners of the entity because they have been insulated from personal liability.

So how does the tenant protect itself? It can seek a guaranty from the owners of the landlord entity, but don't hold your breath. It can seek a non-disturbance agreement (discussed in detail starting on page 106) from the lender (or ground lessor, if there is one), but a small tenant might not get one, or it can buy title insurance insuring its leasehold estate (since a lease creates an interest in the real estate). Title insurance is certainly a necessity for ground leases or for other long-term leases that are critical for the tenant, but it involves expense and delay. Further, it only protects the tenant against prior claimants and not against any future foreclosure or other claim arising thereafter. If there is to be title insurance for the tenant, the lease should be conditioned on the tenant's obtaining it.

Enough said about this provision. Let's move on to something more interesting.

Defaults and Remedies

Tenant's Defaults and Landlord's Remedies

Although many lease forms list numerous events as tenant defaults or events of default, the principal concerns of the landlord are the payment of monthly rent, the payment of additional charges, tenant's carrying the insurance required of it under the lease, and the performance of the other specified obligations of the tenant under the lease. The lease may also deal with insolvency events by the tenant and may even seek to make repeated defaults an event of default that could trigger the landlord's remedies.

I have referred to defaults and events of default. Leases try to deal with the fact that if, for example, the tenant does not pay its rent by the first of the month if required to do so under the lease, it is in default or breach, but if the lease provides that the tenant has a period of time thereafter, or after notice, to cure the failure to pay, the landlord does not have any remedies until it has given the notice, if required, and the time to cure has elapsed. Leases often refer to the failure to pay as a "default" and the failure to pay after the time to cure as a "Default" or an "Event of Default." In that way, these have become defined terms.

Payment of rent is, of course, critical to the landlord. Without prompt payment, the landlord might default under its mortgage or be unable to meet its other obligations, or even be unable to make distributions to its investors. Still, most leases give the tenant a cure period, such as five days. Tenants often argue for longer cure periods. Many leases give a cure period, but do not tie it to the giving of notice. That, to me, is unfair. It severely penalizes the tenant who does not know that its check, which may have been sent on time, has not arrived. Landlords sometimes agree to give notice one or two times a year, after which the tenant may be at risk. It is not illogical, although it is not such a great burden on landlords to give a notice. My lease forms just provide for five days after notice to cure. On the other hand, my lease form contains a repeated default clause.

Many leases provide that the failure to pay the rent on time causes interest to be payable at a default rate. The default rate may be a set amount or an amount tied to some external rate, such as the prime rate as published in the *Wall Street Journal* or some other business publication. Leases used to provide for a default rate of 7% per annum, but in the early 1980s, prime rate rose to over 20%, so the default rate was a bargain. As this is being written, prime is extremely low, so 7% would be tantamount to a penalty rate. Usually when the prime rate is referred to, the default rate is prime plus some additional percentage, such as prime plus 4%, changing as prime changes. The additional percentage is often the subject of negotiation.

Some leases may provide for a late fee in the event of a default in the payment of rent. The landlord must not be too greedy because a very substantial late fee may be deemed to be a penalty and unenforceable. A late fee of 5% of the delinquent payment is pretty common, but other amounts are often negotiated. Tenants often seek a grace period before these charges kick in, and sometimes those are granted, but they, too, may be limited to a specified number in a year.

This is a touchy subject. Hard as it may be to believe, at a time of recession or slow economic growth, but with high inflation and high interest rates, many large companies deliberately paid their rents late so they would have the use of the money or be able to earn interest on it during the grace period. Landlords who know that history want to make certain it does not repeat itself.

As to other obligations of the tenant, a cure period of 30 days is pretty common. Exceptions might be the cure period for keeping the insurance in effect, or for providing documents required for the landlord to obtain its financing, or for dealing with emergency situations, which might be considerably shorter. As to non-payment defaults that cannot with due diligence be cured within 30 days, the tenant is (or should be) allowed additional time to cure, provided it commenced promptly and proceeds diligently to cure. I do not understand why a time limit (such as "not to exceed 60 days") is sometimes inserted. Is the landlord interested in having the problem cured or in having a lawsuit against the tenant? Some cures, such as roof replacement, may not be feasible during the winter.

The remedies available for uncured Defaults or Events of Default vary from jurisdiction to jurisdiction, so it is impossible to enumerate them here. In Illinois, where I practice, the landlord may simply sue for the rent, leaving the tenant in possession of the premises and bound to perform all of its obligations under its lease. On the other hand, the landlord may terminate the tenant's right to possession of the premises without terminating the lease and continue to collect the rent unless the premises are relet (and then still collect any shortfall). And the landlord may, in the alternative, terminate the lease and collect damages, being the difference between the rent specified in the lease and the fair rental value of the premises, each for the balance of the term (but subject to a discount rate). Illinois also provides a statutory duty to mitigate damages,[14] which I know does not exist in all states. Leasing lawyers should become aware of the remedies permitted and generally provided for in leases pertaining to their states.

Most leases also provide that the landlord has the right to cure the tenant's default, and the cost becomes additional rent due from the tenant to the landlord, with interest at some specified default rate. The tenant will, of course, be concerned about the cost and will seek to limit the expenditure to a "reasonable cost" standard. On the other hand, the landlord does not want to have to litigate the reasonableness of the cost and may seek to make it "actual cost," perhaps with a good faith standard (which might involve the landlord in litigation anyway).

Many leases provide very extensive and specific remedies in the event of a bankruptcy. Because the bankruptcy court will determine remedies irrespective of the provisions of the lease, it is my view that those provisions may pretty safely be ignored.

Landlord's Defaults and Tenant's Remedies

Most leases are silent on the subject of the tenant's remedies for the landlord's defaults. This is not surprising because most leases are written, initially at least, by landlords. Most states adhere to the rule that, unlike in contracts generally, if the landlord defaults, the tenant does not have the right to terminate the lease except in the case of "constructive eviction," which occurs when the landlord's default permanently prevents the tenant from operating in the premises. In that regard, the courts follow an ancient rule in real estate lease cases that the obligations agreed to by the tenant (referred to as "independent covenants") are independent of the landlord's obligations

---

14. 735 ILCS 5/9-213.1.

and that the tenant's remedy, in the absence of express language in the lease, is to sue the landlord for damages.

Some tenants, especially major tenants with a lot of clout, get a right to cure the landlord's default. The way it usually works is that if the landlord does not cure within 30 days (shorter in an emergency), the tenant has the right to cure at the landlord's expense. When representing a landlord, I usually seek an additional five-day notice before the tenant begins to cure because the landlord may have contracted for the cure, and the landlord does not want the tenant to do so and cause the landlord to have to pay twice. Many, but not all, leases that include the tenant's right to cure (sometimes referred to as "self-help") provide that if the landlord does not pay the cost of the cure within a specified period, the tenant has the right to deduct (or set-off) the cost from rent thereafter payable. Of course, landlords will resist that. If the landlord cannot avoid the deduction, it may seek to limit the deduction right to base rent (so it has the funds to pay taxes and other pass-through items), or even to a percentage of base rent (so the landlord has the funds to pay its debt service). As in the case of the landlord curing the tenant's default, the landlord will want to ensure that the tenant's cost of curing is controlled.

If the landlord has several tenants on the property that desire self-help remedies, it must be very careful. The last thing the landlord wants is for more than one tenant to contract for snow removal or roof repair. Once the landlord has granted a tenant such a remedy as to common areas, it should advise subsequent tenants to work with the tenant who already has the right to cure.

Security Deposits

The irony of security deposits is that the landlord always needs the most from the tenant that can least afford to pay one. Sometimes the problem is solved by having principals of the tenant post the security, especially if the security deposit is in the form of a letter of credit (see page 91).

Actually, the landlord would like a security deposit from each tenant, even the ones with excellent credit. Why? Because many tenants, even ones with great credit, damage premises or surrender them other than in the condition required in the lease. Also, as we learned during the recession of 2008, many companies we thought were strong turned out not to be. Who would ever have thought that a security deposit from General Motors Corporation would really be needed?

Some landlords typically ask for a security deposit based on one, two, or three months' rent. That, in my judgment, is pretty short-sighted. The security deposit should actually be determined based on the amount of the landlord's risk. Obviously, the landlord should seek a more substantial security deposit from a weak tenant than a strong one. It is not unusual, in the case of a substantial security deposit, to provide for its reduction as the risk to the landlord decreases, provided the tenant is not in default.

In addition, I have already discussed the situation where the landlord did special construction for a tenant and needed assurance that the funds were available if that special construction had to be removed to make the premises usable by a subsequent tenant (see page 10). The landlord may be making a large landlord contribution toward the tenant's improvements and want to know it can recover the unamortized portion of that expense (as well as its brokers' commissions) if the tenant defaults during the term.

Sometimes landlords accept a guaranty instead of a security deposit or reduce the amount of the security deposit based on a guaranty. I will discuss guaranties below (see page 94).

The security deposit section should provide, as it typically does, that the landlord can apply all or a portion of the security deposit to cure defaults. Some sections also provide that the security deposit may be applied to "damages," which makes the landlord, rather than a court, the judge of the amount of damages; when representing a tenant, I argue that such a provision is inappropriate. The section customarily goes on to require the tenant to restore the security deposit to its prior amount in the event of an application. The section may permit commingling of the security deposit with the landlord's other funds and not provide for interest, both of which provisions may be problematic for tenants and, in some states, may not even be permitted. In addition, the section should specify the length of time after the lease expires when the security deposit is to be returned.

It is an open secret, but not necessarily known to tenants, that the real reason the landlord wants a security deposit from every tenant is because it needs the funds to pay the security deposit back to the prior tenant, or to pay the commission, or to pay for construction. That being the case, the right to commingle could be a problem when it comes to getting the security deposit back when the lease expires. There is a further issue of what right the tenant has in commingled funds if the landlord is in bankruptcy.

Letters of Credit

Oddly enough, except for small security deposits, the landlord and the tenant both have advantages from having the security deposit held in the form of a letter of credit. Although the landlord will not be able to use the security deposit for other purposes (which is not very legitimate anyway), the letter of credit gives the landlord a very substantial advantage: If it holds a letter of credit and the tenant goes into bankruptcy, the landlord may draw on the letter of credit and apply the funds as provided in the security deposit section. The thing to be mindful of is that for a period of time after the filing of a bankruptcy, all parties dealing with the bankrupt parties are subject to an automatic stay, which prevents them from doing any act affecting the bankrupt party. They may not even give a notice of default to the bankrupt party, even if the bankrupt party is actually in default. That is why the landlord may not agree to give a notice of default to the tenant before drawing on the letter of credit because it may not be permitted to give that notice and thus is prohibited by the terms of the lease from drawing on the letter of credit until the automatic stay is lifted and the notice may be given, thus losing a great advantage. Since the bank issuing the letter of credit, and not the tenant, is the debtor under that letter of credit, the automatic stay does not prevent the landlord from drawing on the letter of credit and using it as provided in the lease. It is the bank that is prohibited from using the security posted by the tenant to secure the issuance of the letter of credit, at least until the automatic stay is lifted. If the tenant is concerned about the lack of notice before the draw, a compromise might be for the landlord to be obligated to give the notice unless it is prevented from doing so by an automatic stay, in which case the notice would not be required.

An important issue for the landlord is that the bank issuing the letter of credit be sound financially. If the issuing bank becomes insolvent, neither the FDIC nor a bank acquiring the assets of the insolvent bank can be required to honor the letter of credit. Another important issue is to ensure that the letter of credit is in effect as long as the security deposit is to be made in accordance with the lease. A way of ensuring that is to require an "evergreen" letter of credit, which renews automatically unless the issuing bank gives advance notice that it will not be renewed, in which case the language of the lease, as well as the letter of credit, should permit the landlord to draw on the letter of credit before it actually expires.

The landlord will want to make certain that the security deposit can be held for a sufficient period after the lease expires to enable the landlord to use the proceeds to make repairs required by the tenant's acts or omissions or to pay for the removal of property abandoned by tenant. In addition, if rent must be returned to a trustee or debtor in possession because it is deemed a preference under the bankruptcy code, the landlord needs to hold the security deposit (or have the letter of credit to continue in effect) so it can recapture that returned rent from the security deposit (or the proceeds of the letter of credit). Since the period within which a preference repayment may be required under the bankruptcy code is, at this writing, 90 days, the return of the security deposit should occur 100 days after the lease expires (giving the landlord a ten-day grace period). Since that is a long period for the landlord to hold the security deposit, the tenant may request that the lease provide that if the tenant establishes that the conditions which allow a preference do not exist, the security deposit will be returned within 30 days. That is a reasonable request.

Note that the tenant will be required to give security to the bank in order for the bank to issue the letter of credit and will have to pay a fee to the bank for that letter. Still, the advantage for the tenant is the assurance that the letter of credit will expire around the end of the term and it will not have to chase a landlord that may be insolvent for the return of its cash security deposit.

Lawyers representing landlords that require letters of credit should be aware that banks charge the beneficiary of the letter of credit (i.e., the landlord) a substantial amount (such as .25% of the amount of the letter of credit, with a hefty minimum) if the letter of credit is transferred to another beneficiary, as would occur if the property is sold. If the landlord, in negotiating the lease, states that it will pay no more than, say, $100 for a transfer, this puts the onus on the tenant to negotiate a reduced fee with its bank. It should be clear in the negotiations that any fee in excess of the amount specified in the lease will have to be paid by the tenant. That often results in some flexibility by the issuing bank, since it is a charge made with little or no corresponding cost to the bank.

Other Non-Cash Security Deposits

On occasion, I have seen tenants ask that the security deposit be in the form of a bond or that the tenant be allowed to deposit securities instead of cash. Neither of these is a good idea.

Perhaps the tenant will not have to deposit security with the bonding company as it would with a bank, but it will have to have sufficient credit so that it is "bondable," and the cost of the bond will be a lot more than the cost of a letter of credit. The landlord should have a serious problem with the bond, too, because unlike the letter of credit, which must be paid within 24 or 48 hours after a draw, the bonding company is under no compulsion to pay promptly, and it may even take a lawsuit to get paid, especially if the tenant is insolvent.

The problem with the posting of securities, other than the risk of decline in value, is that it takes a great deal of documentation to accomplish that, so that both parties are protected.

Guaranties

A security deposit is better for the landlord than a guaranty, provided that it is sufficient in amount to ensure performance of the lease obligations of the tenant. Still, there are numerous reasons for a landlord to insist on a guaranty, whether or not a security deposit is provided. First, it gives the landlord another bite at the apple if for some reason the tenant does not or cannot perform. Second, unless it is specifically limited, it guaranties all the obligations under the lease. Third, the landlord may, in a properly drafted guaranty, proceed against the guarantor even if the tenant is in bankruptcy.

I discussed above the situation where a tenant is a subsidiary of another company and does not have its own financial statement (see page 33). The parent company will almost always be in a better financial position than the subsidiary, so its guaranty will fill the gap in credit. In another situation, the tenant may be a start-up with no established credit. If the principal of the tenant, either an individual, a group of individuals, or another company, does have a decent financial statement, that party or parties may be asked to sign a guaranty to ensure performance.

Just what does a guaranty provide? If it is a payment and performance guaranty, as is typically used, the guarantor will undertake to make all payments and perform all of the obligations of the tenant. The landlord will generally insist that the guaranty be primary, which is to say that the landlord is not required to exhaust its remedies against the tenant before proceeding against the guarantor. The guarantor will agree to pay all the costs of enforcing the guaranty and will agree that, if the tenant pays rent but the landlord must pay that rent over to a bankruptcy trustee (because the payment was a preference), the guarantor will reimburse the landlord.

The guaranty will generally require that the guarantor waive the right to any notice of default. This certainly appears unfair. However, the reason is that, since guaranties are very strictly construed to protect the guarantor, there is a risk to the landlord that if it misses giving a notice, the entire guaranty may become unenforceable. A compromise position on that issue might be to provide that if the notice is missed, the guarantor cannot collect as to that default, but the guaranty remains in effect as to other defaults as to which notice is given. I have used that language and I hope it is enforceable, but I have never seen it litigated.

The guaranty will also generally require the guarantor to waive any other defenses it might have, but I have gotten landlords to limit the waiver to what is called "suretyship defenses," which are defenses pertaining to guaranties only.

If one entity guaranties the obligations of another, there is always an issue as to whether there is a sufficient relationship between the parties because, unless there is such a relationship or the guarantor receives consideration for giving the guaranty, the guarantor may have a defense against an action seeking to collect on the guaranty. The guaranty may be "ultra vires," or beyond the corporate or other legal power of the guarantor.

I have been involved in situations where an American subsidiary of a major foreign entity negotiates a lease in the United States and, because the American subsidiary does not have adequate credit, the guaranty of the foreign entity is required. That presents some serious special problems. If the guarantor is a company incorporated or organized in the United States, it can be sued somewhere in the United States, either in its principal place of business, in the state of its incorporation or organization, or in some state (including the one where the premises are located) where it is doing business. If the landlord is in a state other than the guarantor's, and the amount at issue exceeds the specified statutory limit, the action may be brought in the Federal District Court where either the plaintiff or the defendant resides. In any case, if a judgment is obtained, it is entitled to "full faith and credit," which means that, once the judgment is registered in other states, it is readily enforceable against assets of the guarantor located in those states.

If, on the other hand, the guarantor is incorporated in a foreign country, the situation is much more complicated. First, there is a question as to whether the foreign guarantor must be sued in its own country, which would be exceedingly inconvenient or, on the other hand, whether it can be sued where the property is located. The guaranty should specify that the guarantor agree that it may be sued in a court where the property is located. Second, there is a concern as to how the guarantor may be brought into that court. Usually a case is commenced by the filing of a Complaint, after which the clerk of the court issues a summons that is served by the sheriff or other official, either directly at the office of the defendant or of a company or individual named as the registered agent for the defendant. Thus, the foreign guarantor should designate a party in the area where the agreed-to court is located to accept service of a summons on behalf of the guarantor. If it or its American subsidiary has no office in that state, it may designate the secretary of state of that state to accept that service. Third, the guaranty should specify that the law of the state where the premises are located is the governing law relative to the guaranty; the parties do not want the law of the foreign country to control.

Finally, assuming a judgment is entered against the guarantor where the property is located, how is it to be collected when the guarantor's assets are in a foreign country? That is a tricky question because the chances are that neither the lawyer representing the landlord nor a local counsel representing the tenant is familiar with the law of that country. What I generally do is request that the guarantor deliver a legal opinion from an attorney licensed in the foreign country that states that the guaranty is duly executed and delivered and is binding on the guarantor, and that a judgment obtained in the court in the United States is enforceable in the foreign country without having to retry the factual issues in the case. I have received such opinions, and some of them have been qualified. The qualifications provided important information. For example, I received an opinion from a German lawyer stating that the judgment was enforceable if no pre-trial discovery was conducted. Discovery was (and perhaps still is) against public policy in Germany. That was extremely important to know because it would govern how litigation against the guarantor was conducted in the United States, discovery being very routine here.

Of course, the guaranty may come from an individual or group of individuals, and not an entity. The issues with foreign individuals are the same as with entities. I just want to note that if the principal asset of an individual guarantor is his or her home, the landlord may have great hesitation to enforce the guaranty and put the guarantor and his or her family on the street. In fact, depending on how the home is owned, that remedy might not even be available.

I have seen tenants offer a "payment guaranty," limiting the landlord's remedy to collect from the guarantor only if the landlord has exhausted its remedies against the tenant (in court) and has been unable to collect from the tenant. That could involve the landlord in extensive litigation against a defaulting tenant (including appeals and actions to collect), which makes the guaranty somewhat useless. At least such a guaranty should provide that the guarantor is obligated to pay the legal fees of the landlord in the litigation against the tenant.

Other Security

Many landlords seek a security interest in their tenants' personal property. In some states, statutory law provides such security interests unless they are expressly waived by the landlord. No such law applies in my state of Illinois, but often leases require that security. If it is provided for in the lease, the landlord will have to "perfect" the security interest by filing a financing statement as required by the Uniform Commercial Code in effect in that state. If it does not do so it may be subject to the rights of later creditors who take a security interest and do file, or it may be subject to bona fide purchasers of the personal property for value without notice of the security interest.

Tenants typically object to granting security interests in their personal property because that can really affect their ability to do business in that property. Of course, a retailer or wholesaler does not want to pledge its merchandise because that would complicate its sale. Even pledging (which is a shorthand way of referring to the granting of a security interest) its furniture, furnishings, and equipment can hurt it, especially if it wants to borrow from a bank or other lending institution based on the value of that property. A very serious problem could arise if the pledge includes property such as computer software and computer programs developed by the tenant; if the landlord realizes on that security, it could ruin the tenant's ability to do business.

As I mentioned, tenants sometimes borrow money from third parties and, to secure those loans, grant a security interest in personal property, including property located in the premises. The lender will often require a waiver from the landlord of any rights the landlord has or may obtain in the pledged property. The landlord may object to certain provisions in the waiver document, or it may not want to waive at all. It is wise for lawyers to address this issue during the lease negotiations. Some landlords' lawyers have a form of Landlord's Waiver that has been, with some modifications, accepted by lenders in the past and that can be attached as an exhibit to the lease. I do.

Some states, including Illinois, have a statute that permits landlords to "distrain for rent." That means that, even before a judgment, the landlord can seize property of the tenant anywhere in the county to pay money claimed to be owed to the landlord. The landlord typically enters the premises, even if it has to break the lock, takes an inventory of what is located there, and padlocks the door. The landlord must then file an action called a "distraint for rent," attaching the inventory to the complaint filed with the court. The landlord cannot seize property in which third parties have an interest, such as other lenders, but that can be worked out after the seizure.

This course is pretty dangerous for landlords because tenants often complain that the landlord stole their property. My former partner joked that one must enter with three men of the cloth to act as witnesses that nothing was taken. This is not a common event, but it is still wise for a lawyer representing a tenant in a state with such a remedy to request that the lease provide that the right to distrain is waived.

Environmental Issues

Although environmental issues are most concerning to landlords and tenants in the case of industrial/warehouse lease situations (because the chemicals used in a manufacturing process or stored in warehouses may, if not used or stored in accordance with environmental laws, create substantial liability for both parties) environmental problems may arise in any of the other leasing situations. A medical facility may generate unhealthy hazardous materials. Even a retail facility may be problematic, especially if it is selling home maintenance and repair items or if it is an automobile dealership with a service center. Certainly gas stations have been prime polluters.

From the tenant's point of view, it is concerned that it may be moving into a facility whose environmental history is problematic. The landlord may not know what its property was used for before, and certainly the tenant may have no better information. Of course, the landlord may have an environmental assessment (unless it has owned the property since before the passage of environmental legislation[15] and has not refinanced since that

---

15. The Comprehensive Environmental Response, Compensation and Liability Act (CER-CLA) was passed in 1980.

time), but that assessment may not be complete or accurate. Still, from the tenant's point of view, the landlord should assume the risk of liability arising from the environmental condition of the property existing at the time the lease is entered into. What is generally negotiated is that the landlord is responsible for remediation (except in ground lease and certain net lease situations, where the tenant must perform environmental testing as a condition of going forward with the lease, or the lease is to be totally "as-is, where-is" and the environmental liability is expressly placed on the tenant). The lease may even contain an indemnity from the landlord for other related liabilities, but landlords strenuously contest that.

In most other lease situations, the tenant makes certain agreements about not using hazardous materials, and if it does so, it is obligated to comply with good management practices and certainly to comply with applicable environmental laws and ordinances. It may have to indemnify the landlord for damages resulting from liability caused by the tenant's violation of such laws, but the tenant is generally only liable for what it causes.

Even there, however, there is a wrinkle. What if hazardous materials then exist in the ground, but not in sufficient quantity or concentration to constitute a violation of law? Along comes the tenant and adds to the hazardous materials. The amount added is not, in itself, enough to constitute a violation, but because it is contributing to what already existed, a violation is created. Some landlords provide that such a contribution causing a violation where none existed before imposes the duty on the tenant to remediate.

Indemnities

Most leases require the tenant to indemnify the landlord for certain specified exposures of the landlord. One of the most common indemnities is in the area of liability for personal injury or property damage. That type of indemnity is included in the discussion of insurance (see page 52). However, there are other situations in which indemnities may be appropriate.

Under an indemnity agreement, one party agrees to take on liability for costs payable to third parties. Sometimes the landlord's lease form requires the tenant to indemnify the landlord for the tenant's default under the lease.

That is not necessary or even appropriate since the landlord already has remedies against the tenant for its default, and the lease probably provides that the losing party is required to pay the attorneys' fee and other expenses of the winner. Similarly, the tenant has remedies against the landlord if the landlord defaults.

Under what circumstances, other than in the insurance situation, might the tenant have liability to third parties?

One example is the circumstance where the tenant hires a contractor to do construction or alterations and fails to pay the contractor. Because the contractor may have a right to file or record a mechanic's lien claim, this is a particularly delicate matter. The lease probably requires the tenant to pay for any construction or alterations it performs in the premises and the failure to do so is a default. However, leases frequently provide indemnities in that situation to ensure that the tenant is obligated to reimburse the landlord for what it is required to pay, including the landlord's costs of defense or the contractor's costs for which the landlord is held liable. It may be "belt and suspenders," but indemnities are commonly provided for in that situation.

Another example is the indemnity for environmental liability. That liability might be for the cleanup of a spill, for a penalty imposed on the landlord, or even for loss of income by the landlord if an adjoining tenant cannot operate or vacates because of the existence of the environmental condition.

A further situation is the holdover by the tenant after the lease expires. If there is another tenant waiting to occupy the space and the landlord is liable to that tenant, either for that tenant's costs resulting from the delay or as a penalty, the landlord will want the tenant holding over to reimburse it for those costs, irrespective of other remedies available to the landlord.

Similarly, if the tenant does not disclose that it has a broker and the landlord becomes obligated to pay an unanticipated commission, the landlord will seek to recover that commission from the tenant pursuant to an indemnity. There may be a warranty by the tenant that it dealt with no broker, and that would give the landlord an adequate remedy, but the landlord will probably feel more secure with an indemnity.

Indemnities may simply require the tenant to reimburse the landlord for any damages and costs, or they may specify that the landlord has the right to retain counsel and to control any litigation or arbitration, all at the tenant's expense.

Sometimes tenants request indemnities from landlords. Such indemnities are probably appropriate to deal with some situations. If, for example, there are pre-existing environmental problems with the premises and the tenant is required to remediate, the tenant would want the right to be reimbursed for its costs. Any landlord indemnity should be carefully drafted. Otherwise, the landlord may find that it is required to indemnify the tenant for the same event or condition for which the tenant is required to indemnify the landlord, and it cannot be determined which party is actually liable.

Estoppel Certificates and SNDAs

What is an estoppel certificate, and why is it grouped in this discussion with something referred to as an SNDA?

Estoppel Certificates

The legal definition of *estop* is to stop, bar, or impede. When a party signs an estoppel certificate, it is barred from denying the accuracy of the matters stated in that certificate. Nearly all leases require the tenant to provide a signed estoppel certificate upon the landlord's request. Sometimes a form of estoppel is attached to the lease, although a lender or buyer may request certifications in addition to the ones referred to in the lease or attached as an exhibit.

Why would a landlord require an estoppel certificate? If the landlord is closing a new mortgage on the property within which the premises are located, the lender will want to make certain that the information the landlord/borrower has provided about the leases is accurate and that there are no claims against the landlord that may adversely affect the value of its collateral or create a possible claim against the lender if it forecloses. Likewise, a prospective buyer will want the same certainty before it closes the purchase.

Note that a tenant mortgaging its interest in the property (its leasehold estate) or assigning its lease, possibly in connection with the sale of its business, will want the right to require the landlord to issue its own estoppel certificate to confirm the truth of matters pertaining to the tenant's right to the interest being mortgaged or sold. It should also be borne in mind that if the estoppel certificate is addressed to the landlord as well as to the lender or prospective purchaser, the landlord may have the right to rely on it even if the facts stated are inaccurate.

Unfortunately, you as the lawyer for the tenant may or may not be consulted when the tenant or landlord is asked to sign an estoppel certificate. Therefore, it is incumbent on you to make certain at the time the lease is entered into that the client understands the importance of checking the accuracy of each statement when an estoppel is requested, because an inaccurate statement will be binding on the client. The client should feel free to revise the document delivered to it to make it accurate.

A typical estoppel requested from a tenant will seek the following confirmations (about which I will comment in italics):

1. Tenant is in full and complete possession of the Premises demised under the Lease, such possession having been delivered by the Landlord pursuant to the Lease and having been accepted by Tenant. The improvements to the Premises that Landlord is required to furnish under the Lease have been completed in all respects to the satisfaction of Tenant, and the Premises are open for the use of Tenant, its customers, employees and invitees. *If work to be performed by the landlord has not been completed or is not satisfactory, the defects should be itemized, and if the tenant is not certain of all the defects, it should state that fact or that the defects are only the ones that have been discovered at the time of the delivery of the estoppel. If the premises are not open for business, that should be stated.*

2. All contributions required to be paid by Landlord to Tenant in connection with improvements to the Premises have been paid in full. *This one is very important because if this is not true but that is not disclosed, the tenant will not have the right to collect from the lender (after foreclosure) or from the buyer.*

3. All duties or obligations of Landlord required under the Lease which were an inducement to Tenant to enter into the Lease have been fully performed. *The comment to item 2 applies here, too.*

4. The Lease is in full force and effect. No default exists on the part of Landlord or Tenant under the Lease, nor does any circumstance currently exist that, but for the giving of notice or the passage of time, or both, would be such a default. *This is a trap. Generally, the tenant does not know if the landlord has actually performed all of its obligations, so it should qualify this statement with "to its knowledge."* The Lease constitutes the entire rental agreement between Landlord and Tenant with respect to the Premises and has not been amended, modified, or supplemented, except as attached hereto. *All amendments should be attached or referred to.* There are no oral agreements between Landlord and Tenant with respect to the Premises. *Disclose any.* A true and correct copy of the Lease (including all amendments thereto) is attached to this Certificate *(this can be a nuisance—a reference to the lease should suffice, especially if there are many exhibits attached)* and Tenant agrees not to amend or modify the Lease without the prior written consent of Lender *(an estoppel certificate should not impose obligations on the tenant which are not contained in the lease—they are likely to be forgotten).*

5. No rents under the Lease have been prepaid, except the current month's rent. Tenant agrees that it shall not prepay any rents under the Lease more than one month from the date when such rents are due. *This is okay, if true. Sometimes landlords require payment of the first month's rent when the lease is signed, even though the rent commencement date may not occur until leasehold improvements are finished or a rent-free period has elapsed.* Tenant does not now have or hold any claim or defense against Landlord which might be set off or credited against future accruing rents or which might otherwise excuse Tenant's performance under the Lease. *Any concessions, tenant improvement allowances, or other credits should be listed.*

6. Tenant has received no notice of a prior sale, transfer, assignment, or pledge of the Lease or of the rents secured therein. *There may be an existing mortgage that is being paid off. The tenant should disclose any of which it has received notice.*

7. Tenant does not have any outstanding options or rights of first refusal to purchase the Premises, or any part thereof, or to purchase or lease

any other part of the Building, except (state none, if applicable) *be disclosed if they exist.*

8. No actions, whether voluntary or involuntary, are pending against Tenant or any guarantor of the Lease under any bankruptcy, insolvency or similar laws of the United States or any state thereof. *Okay if accurate.*

9. The term of the Lease commenced on the ____ day of _____, 20__ and ends on the ____ day of _____, 20__, subject to options to extend, if any, set forth in the Lease. *Insert the accurate information.*

10. The current monthly base rental payable by Tenant under the Lease is $_____. Percentage rent [is/is not] payable, as provided in the Lease. The current estimated monthly payments made by Tenant under the Lease in respect of common area maintenance costs and real estate taxes are $_____ and $_____, respectively. *Insert the accurate information.*

11. The security deposit under the Lease is currently $_____. Insert the accurate information or insert "None" if there is no security deposit.

12. So long as the Loan is outstanding, Tenant shall pay any termination fees payable for the early termination of the Lease to Landlord and Lender jointly. *An estoppel certificate should not contain new obligations of the tenant—they are likely to be forgotten.*

13. Lender will rely on the representations and agreements made by Tenant herein in connection with Lender's agreement to make the Loan and Tenant agrees that Lender may so rely on such representations and agreements. *This is merely a reminder of the effect of the estoppel certificate.*

Leases sometimes seek to deal with the situation where the tenant does not promptly sign and return the estoppel certificate. I can attest to the fact that if the landlord is financing or selling a property with many tenants, collecting all of the estoppel certificates on a timely basis can be quite a chore. However, the remedies inserted into the leases can be very onerous. One common remedy is that if the estoppel certificate is not returned within the time specified in the lease, the tenant is deemed to have confirmed all of the statements in the document. Another remedy, which has pretty much the same effect, is that the landlord is authorized to sign the document on the tenant's behalf. With due regard for the landlord's problem, I submit that those remedies should be unacceptable to the tenant.

It should be noted that the estoppel certificates are customarily delivered by the tenant to the landlord, not directly to the lender or to the buyer. There is a good reason for the landlord to want that to happen. A tenant may make a statement that is not true or have a claim the landlord is willing to remedy right away. If the document is delivered to the lender or buyer, it may cause serious problems that a conversation between the landlord and tenant could have avoided. On the other hand, if a landlord who is not very scrupulous receives an estoppel certificate with statements that may hinder its deal, it may be tempted to throw the estoppel certificate in the recycling bin, claim it was never returned and either sign the original one or take the position with the lender or the buyer that the facts were all admitted.

In representing a lender or buyer who was asked to accept such a document or rely on the lease language that the facts were admitted, I would recommend that it not do so. But who can be certain that the lender or buyer would get or decide to accept that advice? I admit that it is difficult to fashion a remedy for the default in delivering an estoppel certificate, but from a tenant's point of view, the ones described above are not acceptable, and the operative language should be deleted from the lease.

SNDAs

SNDA is short for Subordination and Non-Disturbance Agreement. If a property leased before a mortgage was in place is later being financed, or if the landlord is refinancing a prior mortgage, then in addition to the estoppel certificate, the lender may well ask for an SNDA. In that connection the important concept to know and remember is as follows: *If the lease is executed and delivered before the mortgage is, and the mortgagee has notice (by recording of a memorandum of lease) or actual knowledge of the existence of the lease (such as by inspecting the property and seeing the tenant building out the space or conducting its business), the lease has priority, and if there is a foreclosure, the lender cannot wipe out the lease.*

A new lender may not be concerned about the tenant's being protected against foreclosure, but the lender has some legitimate concerns that may require the tenant's agreement. For example, it may want the agreements referred to in the estoppel certificate to which I objected in italics. It may also want to know that it, rather than the tenant, has the first claims in the event of a casualty loss or a condemnation. Most importantly, however, it will want the tenant to agree to attorn to it in the event of a foreclosure, as discussed on page 74. For those reasons, the lender may want the tenant to subordinate its legal position (as first in time, first in right), but at the same time, the lender will agree to the non-disturbance and recognition, all as discussed above.

Lease forms often provide that the lease will be subordinate to a subsequent loan, but do not provide for an SNDA from the lender. Some leases state that the tenant will not be disturbed in the event of a foreclosure of a loan by a subsequent lender. Neither of those provisions should satisfy the tenant. The obligation to subordinate should be conditioned on the landlord's obtaining an SNDA from the new lender. The obligation of the tenant to be subordinate is enforceable by the lender, as a third party beneficiary, but the landlord cannot agree to non-disturbance on behalf of a lender—only the lender can agree to that. The landlord's agreement that the tenant will not be disturbed is meaningless. Whom is the tenant going to sue if the property, which is all that is owned by this landlord, is foreclosed?

Even a small tenant should not be required to give up a priority position without the protection, even if somewhat limited, of the SNDA. And the SNDA should be commercially reasonable in form or, for larger tenants, reasonably acceptable to the tenant.

Lease forms often provide that if the tenant does not sign the SNDA presented by the lender, the landlord is authorized to do so, as attorney in fact for the tenant. When representing a tenant, I strongly object to that, not only for the reasons stated above in connection with the estoppel certificate, but also because I object to my tenant clients giving a power of attorney to landlords for any purposes. Just as in the case of the estoppel certificate, the tenant and its counsel should have the right to review and evaluate the agreements that the tenant is being asked to make.

Force Majeure

Force majeure is a French phrase that has the following dictionary definition: "an event or effect that cannot be reasonably anticipated or controlled."[16] As examples, we might list strikes, lockouts, labor trouble (whether legal or illegal), civil disorder, failure of power, restrictive governmental laws and regulations, delays in the issuance of building permits or certificates of occupancy by the appropriate governmental authority, riots, insurrections, war, shortages, accidents, casualties, "acts of God," acts caused directly by the other party or its agents, employees and invitees, or any other cause beyond the reasonable control of a party.

The question is whether the occurrence of any of these events excuses the performance under the lease by the party affected by them. The simple answer is "no"—unless the lease provides that it does.

Let's take an example unrelated to leasing. A farmer plants his wheat crop in the spring, and it starts coming up nicely. Being in need of cash, he enters into a contract to deliver the crop when harvested to the local miller at $5 per bushel. You can figure out what happens next—there is a late summer drought, and most of the crop is destroyed. Will the drought excuse the farmer's obligation to deliver the wheat at $5 per bushel? Not on your life! The poor farmer must go on the market and buy wheat, now at $7 per bushel, to deliver it for $5 per bushel, a loss to him of $2 per bushel (and there are a lot of bushels covered in the contract). The next year, the farmer asks the miller for a provision in the contract that excuses his performance if there is another drought or, perhaps, a flood, or any act of God. "No way!" says the miller. "I need predictability for my business." What does the farmer do? He hedges. He buys a futures contract, which is an option to buy wheat. He covers his delivery, and he may actually make some money by selling that futures contract (if he does not need it) on the Board of Trade.

Well, there are no futures contracts for lease performance, at least not yet. There is insurance against some of the events, such as fire, windstorm,

---

16. http://www.merriam-webster.com/dictionary/force%20majeure.

even flood or earthquake, but not as to many of the other events referred to, so the parties need lease language that has the effect of superseding the general legal principle that force majeure does not excuse performance (or excuse prompt performance). Since most leases are written on forms prepared by landlords, it should not be a great surprise that the party whose performance is most often excused (or delay permitted) is the landlord's.

This is not to say that tenants do not also seek force majeure protection and often get it, but with certain exceptions. Those exceptions are (or should be) the tenant's obligation to pay rent and other charges, provide a security deposit when and if required in the lease, provide evidence of insurance required under the lease, surrender the premises when required, or deliver estoppel certificates and SNDAs when required.

Tenant's Financial Statements

Leases usually contain a requirement that the tenant (and its guarantor, if there is one) deliver to the landlord, from time to time, financial statements (preferably audited and certified, but if those are not customarily prepared, statements certified as true and correct by an executive officer of the tenant) so the landlord can, in turn, deliver them to its lender, or its prospective lenders or purchasers. That seemingly innocuous requirement can and often does create disputes and sometimes even kills deals. Of course, there is no problem for publicly held companies; they are quite willing to deliver their annual statements and their other filings with the Security and Exchange Commission. After all, those materials are available to the general public on the Internet.

With privately held companies or with individual proprietorships, the matter is more problematic. These prospective tenants feel that no one should have the right to see their statements. Their reasons might be that they are afraid the information will reach their competitors, or that their income, expenses, assets, liabilities, and net worth are no one's business but their own. They may even have something to hide, but we should not assume that to be the case.

The issue is sometimes resolved with the landlord's agreement to hold the materials in confidence, although it may deliver them to its lender, prospective lenders, or prospective purchasers. There may be a further condition that the documents be delivered to the landlord or by the landlord to those parties only if they execute a confidentiality agreement stating that they will not show the materials to anyone or disclose their contents except on a need-to-know basis or in the event they are compelled to do so in litigation. I have always wondered about the effectiveness of such agreements. How are they to be enforced? If the tenant knows or suspects that the confidence will be breached, it can sue to enjoin disclosure, but how, in most cases, will it know that? Once the information is disclosed, the cat is out of the bag, as it were. How does a court determine what damages are to be assessed against the revealing party? How does anyone even know who has seen the materials unless the agreement is so tightly written that it does not even pay for the landlord to request the statements?

On occasion, the tenant will agree to deliver the materials, with a confidentiality agreement, directly to the lender or to the prospective lender or purchaser, as the case may be, and not to the landlord at all. The landlord prefers to see the materials before they are delivered to the other party because it can then determine what issues may be raised as a result of the contents and develop a strategy for dealing with those issues. Still, the landlord will usually agree to that condition, even though it may have to discuss problems with a lender or buyer without any knowledge of the basis for the discussion.

Some years ago I had a major deal that nearly cratered on this issue. The tenant simply refused to deliver the material to anyone. Here is how we resolved it: The tenant agreed that the lender or buyer could come to its office where that party would be shown the statements. The lender or buyer could ask questions but not copy any documents or take any notes. Neither party was very satisfied with that compromise, but it enabled the deal to go forward. It is a result that might be helpful to you if you have a deal teetering on the edge of a cliff because of this issue.

Landlord's Expenses

Many leases provide, pretty broadly, that the tenant is to reimburse the landlord for certain expenses (including reasonable attorneys' fees). Those expenses might include those incurred for (a) arbitration or court costs incurred in enforcing the tenant's obligations under the lease; (b) curing any default by the tenant; (c) appearing, defending, or otherwise participating in any action or proceeding arising from the filing, imposition, contesting, discharging, or satisfaction of any lien or claim for lien; or (d) defending or otherwise participating in any legal proceedings initiated by or on behalf of the tenant in which the landlord is not adjudicated to be in default under the lease. Those types of expenses are really pretty unlikely to occur.

On the other hand, the lease may provide for the tenant to pay landlord's expenses incurred in connection with any investigation or review of any conditions or documents in the event the tenant requests the landlord's agreement, approval, or consent to any action of the tenant that may be desired by the tenant or required of the tenant under the lease. The approval or consent provision refers to requests by the tenant for consent to an assignment or sublease or requests for approval of alterations and of the plans and specifications for alterations, both of which might require the landlord to incur costs for outside lawyers or architects. Those types of expenses are certainly more likely to be incurred by landlords and are thus of concern to tenants.

There are two issues in the landlord expenses section that are frequently the subject of negotiation. The first relates to legal fees for defaults. The tenant wants to have its fees and costs reimbursed if it wins the litigation, either because of its having sued the landlord or because it has been sued. This mutuality is usually agreed to in what is typically referred to as "prevailing party" language.

I recently revised my customary lease insert, however, when the following occurred: A landlord client sued a tenant claiming an Event of Default under its lease. Because of some defect in the filing (I did not handle the litigation, but I assure you that I am not immune to mistakes), the suit was dismissed, with the landlord being given leave to refile the case. The tenant argued that, because the case was dismissed at its motion, it was entitled to reimbursement of its fee. The client requested a change in the form (that is how leases grow), and I provided that the reimbursement would occur only if there was a decision on the merits of the case (which there certainly did not occur there and would not have occurred even if the landlord had not had the right to refile the action).

The other issue relates to the reimbursement for the cost of obtaining the landlord's consent. It should be borne in mind that most consents requested under a lease do not involve the landlord in any expense. There are two that do. One is consent relating to construction (actually, that consists of a number of consents—one relating to the right to perform the work and others relating to the plans or approval of contractors). The other consent relates to assignment or subletting. Both of these may involve the landlord in costs for professionals outside its organization. If the landlord incurs out-of-pocket expenses for the sole benefit of the tenant, it feels that the tenant should pay for that. The tenant may be willing to pay something, but is concerned about how much it will cost and how the costs may be controlled. Tenants frequently ask for caps on the amount of the reimbursement. That may be agreeable to a landlord in the case of and assignment or subletting (although the rate of attorneys' fees do increase over time), but not in the case of construction, where the number and complication of the decision to grant or withhold consent may be complicated and time-consuming. A further issue arises if the professionals are inside the landlord's organization, such as in-house counsel. I cannot really recommend an outcome here, as the outcomes vary considerably.

Sometimes the tenant asks for reimbursement if its consent is required, or even if it is required to sign an estoppel certificate or an SNDA. Generally, only strong tenants get the landlord to agree to those.

Surrender

What should the condition of the premises be at the end of the term, whether because the lease has expired, because the lease is terminated early by reason of an agreement between the parties, or by reason of a default? Most leases state that the tenant must remove its furniture, fixtures, and equipment, and repair any damage resulting from the removal. Many also make it the landlord's option as to whether the tenant is to remove its alterations or leave them (unless the landlord has agreed otherwise when the alterations were performed). Some leases provide that if the tenant removes alterations, it must restore the premises to their condition prior to the making of the alterations. After all, the landlord will argue, if the tenant tore out some building fixtures or walls to install its alteration, shouldn't it be required to put the original fixtures or walls back in so that the premises do not need a lot of work by the landlord in order to relet them? On the other hand, the tenant will argue that restoration may be very expensive and the next tenant may not have a need for those fixtures or walls or that the landlord may intend to rip out all the leasehold improvements and alterations anyway. This is a matter that should be resolved by the parties, and perhaps the decision should actually be made when the tenant proposes making an alteration that includes removal of existing fixtures or walls. Of course, the landlord will probably not know at the time the alteration is installed what might be required by a subsequent tenant, but it probably can make a pretty educated guess based on the nature of the proposed alteration.

Then there is the exception for "reasonable wear and tear" or "ordinary wear and tear"—both of which are acceptable, but I prefer "reasonable." Premises get older and wear out even if the tenant performs all the required maintenance, repairs, and replacements. Of course, wear and tear should not be used to enable the tenant to escape the consequences of its default in not maintaining the premises as required under the lease, so some language to that effect may be appropriate. In addition, damage resulting from tenant's particular use of the premises, such as damage resulting from a particular manufacturing process (even if permitted under the lease), should not, from the landlord's point of view, be deemed "reasonable wear and tear."

What about loss by fire or other casualty? If the landlord is obligated under the lease to restore after a casualty loss, then "or loss by fire or other casualty" should be added after "reasonable wear and tear." On the other hand, if the tenant is required to restore, it should not be excused from doing so by reason of the fact that the lease has ended (possibly because the loss occurred toward the end of the term), but the parties might agree, at that time, that the insurance proceeds (plus any shortfall) will be paid over to the landlord in lieu of the tenant's restoration of the premises.

Notices

You may wonder why I consider notices to be so important as to cover the topic in this book. It is because if notices are not received in a timely manner, the party receiving the notice will not have the opportunity to correct the problem of which it is being notified. On the other hand, if one of the parties has a right that it must exercise by giving notice on or before a specific date, and the notice arrives late, the right may be gone.

Notice sections generally provide for various ways to give notice, such as personal delivery, registered or certified mail, commercial courier, or by fax or e-mail with a follow-up notice by mail. I have pretty strong views about mailed notices. If I send them by registered or certified mail, a receipt is required, and if it is to be signed by the addressee only, the postal service might have to make several attempts to deliver. Even if the item can be signed for by any responsible person, I have found that it takes the postal service a long time to get the item to the address and a long time to get the receipt back so the sender knows when the addressee accepted the notice and whether it is effective for its purposes. If receipt or refusal is the trigger (and I believe it should be, except as discussed below, the sender does not know for some time whether the trigger has been pulled and it can act on the fact that the notice is given or deemed given. This will delay the sender's right to file suit, which may have substantial consequences, especially if the recipient has filed for bankruptcy relief before the notice is received. In that situation, not only is the sender subject to the automatic stay (see page 92) but, if the lease has not been effectively terminated due to a default before the filing of the bankruptcy, the lease may be an asset of the bankrupt estate, with considerable bad consequences for the landlord.

A better course, in my view, would be personal delivery (although I am somewhat skeptical about who might actually be doing the delivering and who may actually be the recipient) or commercial courier with receipt. Except in extraordinary circumstances, the notice will be there the next business day and the sender will be able to confirm delivery with very little difficulty.

The exception I mentioned above is the exercise of an option or right, of which notice must be given on or before a specified date. In that case, sending the notice by Federal Express, which may fly the document to Memphis even if the notice is being sent across town, may not get it there by the next business day if there is a major snow storm or other "force majeure" event that keeps its planes out of the sky. I believe that such notices should be effective as of the date they are sent.

What about fax notices? It seems to me that fax is rapidly going out of fashion and may soon be as obsolete as the pony express and, besides, there is no assurance that a notice sent to a common fax machine actually reached the right person. I am not very comfortable with e-mail notices either. Hit a wrong key and the notice is never received by the intended addressee, and the sender will not know it since it may have gone to another person who simply deleted it instead of responding. Another problem is that it may have been missed in the storm of e-mails each of us receives every day, or it may have been blocked by a spam or junk mail filter.

Rent

There are only two things I can think of that are universal to all leases—the provision for the use and occupancy of the premises by the tenant and the payment of rent to the landlord.

The word *rent* covers a lot of payments by the tenant to the landlord, and most leases specify in some way that all rent, additional rent, and other charges are referred to as "rent." That is because many states provide for expedited proceedings to evict defaulting tenants and allow the court in those proceedings to include a judgment for rent. If certain charges are not characterized as "rent," the landlord would have to bring a separate, non-expedited action to collect them.

The specified periodic rent, often referred to as "base rent" or "minimum rent," is set forth in all leases. I will refer to it here as "base rent." Unlike other forms of rent that will be discussed below, the lease provisions dealing with the base rent do not differ based on the type of lease. Annual base rent (and the monthly installments) or monthly base rent is customarily set forth in the lease. If specific periodic increases in base rent have been agreed to as the financial escalation during the initial term or any extensions or expansions (such as percentage increases), those increases are described or the actual amounts set out in a schedule. Other forms of financial escalation are more complicated, as we shall see.

Cost-of-Living Adjustments

Sometimes leases of various types provide for increasing base rent based on increases of the cost of living. The most common way to calculate this information is to use a Consumer Price Index published by the Bureau of Labor Statistics of the United States Department of Labor. It is important to note that the Bureau prepares a number of different indices. For example, there are indices for "All Urban Consumers—CPI-U" and for "Urban Wage Earners and Clerical Workers—CPI-W." Each of those indices is published on a national basis and on regional bases. The lease should specify which index should be used. Then again, the indices have been published over the years with different base years. The base at this writing is 1982 – 84 = 100.

A lease using CPI-U or CPI-W should specify the comparison years or months to be used for calculating the increase in the rent (landlord-drafted leases usually provide that rent is not to be reduced). As the base for that purpose, I usually specify the month that is two months before the beginning of the measuring period and two months before the effective date of the increase. I do that because that will make the rate knowable when the rent bumps up. For example, if the rent is to start on June 1, 2014 and the increase in rent is to occur one year later, I would provide that the CPI for April 2014 should be compared with the CPI for April 2015 to determine the percentage of increase, and so on year by year.

Another possible index is the GDP Deflator, published by the Bureau of Economic Analysis of the United States Department of Commerce. That index compares the levels of Gross Domestic Product between two specified years or months. The drafter of the lease may examine the various indices to determine which one has historically been more favorable to its client, but usually that does not happen, especially on the average lease deal. Generally, one of the CPI-U indices is referred to.

Also, the parties might agree to use a cost-of-living adjustment but to predicate the rent increase on a stated percentage of the increase in the index, such as 50% of the increase during the period. That is a way to compromise the financial escalation.

In the years since the end of high inflation experienced in the 1980s, cost of living adjustments have fallen out of favor and specified increases have become more common. However, one cannot be certain that inflation will be low forever, so we might expect that one day cost of living adjustments will re-emerge in leases. On the other hand, in the year 2010 there was considerable fear of deflation, which has not been experienced in the United States since the Great Depression. Might not some tenants seek a cost of living adjustment to reduce the rent if the applicable index declines?

Market Rent

Sometimes the parties are unable to agree as to what the rent amount should be at some future date. This frequently happens in the case of a ground lease, which generally has a very long term. The situation may also arise where there is an option to extend or an option to lease additional or other premises. The parties may specify that market rent will apply (see page 116, where proposed methods of determining market rent was discussed). Unless the landlord and the tenant are very specific as to what market rent means and how it is to be determined, they may find that instead of specifying a reasonable means of determining the rent, they have created a monster. If the lease only provides that the parties are to agree on the market rent, even if they must act in good faith, they will probably have created what is known at law as "an illusory agreement," which is not enforceable because it is simply an agreement to agree. They can litigate with one another, but the fact remains that no judge is going to want to decide what the rent should be in the given situation.

In order to determine market rent, the parties must first define the "relevant market. This is not as easy as it sounds. Take a retail situation, for example. Assume the tenant is seeking to lease a store on Fifth Avenue and 53rd Street in New York City. How comparable is rent for similar space on 53rd and Lexington Avenue or even Fifth Avenue and 43rd Street? How comparable is the rent for a 1,000-square-foot space on Fifth Avenue and 53rd Street with a 10,000-square-foot space in the same area? Even if the reader is not familiar with New York geography, I think nearly everyone knows that midtown Fifth Avenue is an upscale retail area. Lexington Avenue or south of midtown is not.

Likewise, in an office lease situation, if the space is in a 40-year-old building, how do the rents compare with a new building across the street, let alone in another area of the city? Perhaps the only comparable space is space in the same building, but even there, some tenants have long-term leases and their rents may have been negotiated a long time ago, whereas some are new tenants. And besides, the landlord may be quoting an even higher rent for tenants looking for space when the market rent is to be determined. The situation may be easier in the industrial/warehouse situation, but not necessarily so.

When and if the relevant market is agreed to, there is still the question of what constitutes the "rent." That is not an easy question either. If the tenant is paying rent on a net basis, the question to be answered is fairly straightforward. What is the net rent for the relevant market at the time the market rent is being determined? However, what is the market rent if the tenant is paying a gross base rent and a percentage of certain costs over a base? Remember that in that situation, the base costs are included in the gross base rent at the time the lease is first negotiated. Assume that the gross rent is $25, but the taxes, insurance, and operating expenses (the pass-throughs) included in that gross rent is $10, and that the base is $10. If in 10 years, the market gross rent is $35 because the pass-throughs have increased to $15 (the other $5 is simply a market increase), unless the base for the pass-throughs is increased to $15, the tenant is not really getting a market rate; it is overpaying by $5.

There is yet another variable to be considered: What if other tenants have had concessions? Perhaps they have had some free rent, or they have had new build-out, which is not contemplated in connection with the current deal as to which the new rent is being determined. Landlords are not giving those concessions away for nothing. It is factored into the rent the other tenant will be paying over the balance of its term. In other words, the "comparable rent" is a rent that includes the amortization (with some profit factor) of the concessions. Unless your tenant is to get concessions of similar value, its "market rent" should be reduced by the amount the concessions are being factored into the supposedly comparable rent.

Finally, it is very likely that the landlord would have to pay a commission on a new lease, so the market rate includes a factor for that commission. Unless the broker who represented the tenant was able to get the landlord to agree to pay a commission on extension (which is pretty unusual), the landlord is getting a great deal if it gets a rent that has a commission factored in, but does not have to pay one. That is why you sometimes see that the actual rent is to be 95% of market rent.

All right, let us assume that the parties have agreed to the appropriate market and considered all the factors impacting the rate of rent described above, and they have further agreed that they will attempt in good faith to decide on the applicable rent considering all those matters. What should the lease provide in the event the landlord and tenant are unable to agree on the market rent?

Obviously, some third party or parties will have to make the decision. The parties might agree on arbitration. That is a pretty thorough way to have the decision made. Each party does an investigation of rents in the market, considering all the factors. Then there is an evidentiary hearing before one or more arbitrators (who are paid by the parties), and the decision made by the arbitrator or arbitrators is binding on the parties. The parties will have been represented by lawyers and will have had expert witnesses testify. It would have to be quite a deal to justify all those expenses.

Another approach is to have experts make the decision. Each party hires its own expert and they each render their opinion as to the market rent. Obviously, it is very unlikely that they will come up with the same number, so some method of resolving the difference will still have to be considered.

One alternative is what is called "baseball arbitration." The experts (or even the parties themselves) come up with an amount and a third party (also an expert) decides which is closest to the proper number, and that is the market rent. In an alternative to "baseball arbitration," the lease may provide that if the higher amount is within 10% of the lower amount, the two are averaged for the answer. If not, a third expert, selected by the first two, decides the question.

There is still another issue to be resolved. Who are to be the experts? I have often seen leases that designate appraisers as experts. Well, those people may know how to find comparables to determine value for sale or financing purposes, but they are extremely unlikely to know what the rents are in a given market since that information is not publicly available. Really, only brokers can be expected to know that because they are dealing with those numbers every day. So the parties might designate brokers with a certain level of experience who are unrelated to either party and who have not done business with them; this is the method I prefer.

When all is said and done, when the parties see how long these procedures take, how much the experts will cost, and understand that even at its best, the decision-making process will be flawed, they usually end up agreeing on the market rent themselves.

Some parties may object to a binding determination of market rent. Their thinking is that they don't want to be bound unless they feel that the outcome is fair. Of course, that undermines the entire system created to determine the applicable rent, and if either party has the right to reject the determination, that makes the entire provision, however carefully drafted, illusory.

Taxes

Taxes applicable to the property are a major expense and can increase substantially during the term of a lease. Landlords are very eager to pass that expense on to tenants, either as part of their base rent or as a pass-through, but what taxes should or should not be passed through?

Certainly, real estate taxes are a valid pass-through, but which year's real estate taxes? In states where taxes are paid in the year in which they are assessed, that is a fairly easy question to answer. However, in the state where I practice—Illinois—and in several other states, taxes are assessed on one year and payable the next. In fact, the amount of the 2013 taxes will not even be determined until sometime in 2014, which creates special problems in those states; do the tenants pay based on the taxes that are assessed in a specific year, or based on those that are payable in that year? If payable, the landlord collects less of the taxes it has to pay for the term of the lease; if assessed, the landlord has to figure out how to collect for taxes payable during the year after the lease term has ended. I won't belabor this because it is a problem unique to those states with that crazy system.

Another tax is the special assessment, usually for an improvement performed by the municipality or county, such as a road or alley improvement. Those assessments are usually payable up front or in installments with interest. Landlords look to collect those assessments from the tenants, but the tenants want to pay only those installments that would fall due during the term of their leases, whether the landlord pays up front or not. There may also be special taxes for transportation or sewage or drainage districts, which are customarily included in the definition of taxes. Some jurisdictions have rent taxes, and those are customarily passed on to the tenants. If there are great variations in the amount of rent payable by different tenants, those paying lower rents will want the landlord to bill them for the taxes on their rent, but those paying higher rents will want the landlord to aggregate the rent taxes and charge all the tenants on a pro-rata basis.

Landlords frequently use the tax definition section to provide for the tenant's payment of the cost of contesting the tax assessment; tenants usually seek to limit the amount they are charged to the savings they realize. Tenants will also want to receive their pro rata share of any refund, but how will they ever know there was a refund, especially if it is paid after the lease expires?

There are usually certain exclusions from the definition of taxes. Those are federal income taxes; state or local net income taxes; federal excess profits taxes; franchise, capital stock, and federal or state estate or inheritance taxes of the landlord. Note that gross income taxes are not excluded. There is, however, an exception to the exclusion, which is for taxes that are subsequently imposed on the landlord and are measured by or based in whole or in part on the lease, the premises, the property, or the rent, to the extent that those taxes would be payable if the property were the only property of the landlord.

In many states, property taxes have reached what is considered unacceptable levels, and some day those states may undertake to pay a larger share of local costs out of statewide revenue, particularly for schools. Based on that, new state taxes may be passed with the condition that property taxes be reduced. The purpose of the exception to the exclusions is to make the landlord whole if it pays less property tax but has to pay a substituted or increased income or other state tax. How this will play out if the taxation method is changed as described cannot be predicted with certainty.

Some landlords seek to include a provision in the tax section providing for the grossing up of taxes if the taxes are reduced due to substantial vacancy on the property. Grossing up will be defined and described on page 136.

Tenants sometimes ask for maximums or caps on pass-throughs or on their annual increases. That is understandable, since tenants like to quantify their expenses. The problems for landlords are: (a) Some expenses, such as taxes, insurance, and snow removal, are totally out of the landlord's control; and (b) it is difficult to estimate even the initial cost of items that are nominally within the landlord's control, but that may increase over the term because of inflation or other factors. When one considers that pass-throughs exist to protect landlords from the effects of inflation and that they are supposed to reflect actual costs (and not profit to landlords), caps do not make much sense. However, we can still expect them to be requested and sometimes agreed to by landlords.

Multi-Owner Expenses

If the property containing the premises is part of a larger complex with multiple owners, such as an industrial park, an office park, or a retail center, there is likely to be a Declaration of Easements, Covenants and Restrictions that was recorded by the developer of the park or center and that requires the property owners to pay their share of certain costs, such as the cost of maintenance of landscaping, private roads, common parking areas, storm water retention or detention facilities, private utilities, and the like. Those costs, whether billed directly to the tenant or paid by the landlord and re-billed to the tenant, will be the tenant's expense, as pass-throughs (see page 4).

Energy-Saving Equipment

Although I discussed the issue of including capital expenditures in connection with pass-throughs for various types of properties, the issue of passing through the capital cost of energy-saving equipment is a unique one. Unless the landlord is a substantial user of energy for common areas of the property, such as for an enclosed mall, most of the benefits of installing expensive energy-saving equipment will inure to the benefit of the tenants only. They are the major users of the heating, air conditioning, lighting, and other energy-consuming equipment. Thus, there is what has been referred to as a "split incentive issue." Most people and businesses—including public-relations-minded tenants—are concerned about being "green" these days, and frankly, this is the wave of the foreseeable future. Almost all leases that provide for pass-throughs deal generally with capital improvements, one way or the other, but most such leases do not yet deal with pass-throughs for energy-saving capital improvements. They will.

The New York City Mayor's Office of Long Term Planning and Sustainability convened a working group of major building owners, tenants, property managers, lawyers, and engineers to address the split-incentive issue, and they developed lease language to allocate the cost of those improvements. Suffice it to say that this is a developing area in commercial leasing of multi-tenant buildings where operating expenses or common area expenses are passed through to the tenants.

Abandoned Cables

In 2002, the National Fire Protection Association focused on a substantial problem that existed in all buildings where cables used for communication had been abandoned. Abandoned cable is defined as "installed communications cable that is not terminated at both ends at a connector or other equipment and not identified 'For Future Use' with a tag." Those cables that were located above the ceilings or below the floors, as well as in risers in multi-story buildings, constituted a serious fire hazard, as well as a hazard of toxic gases, if the building containing them caught fire. According to estimates at that time, more than 45 billion feet of plenum cable, much of it looking a lot like a mass of twisted spaghetti, was in place in buildings. Since 2002, the National Electric Code (the "NEC") requires that all abandoned copper and fiber cable be removed. While the NEC requirements do not have the effect of law, a majority of jurisdictions adopt the NEC by reference in local building and fire codes.

While building owners have the ultimate responsibility for the removal of abandoned cable, it can be expected that they may seek to transfer the responsibility to their tenants. On the other hand, landlords may expect tenants to require that abandoned cables be removed as a precondition to the delivery of the premises. Since the NEC was proposed in 2002, much of that cabling has probably already been removed. It is something tenants' brokers should raise in their lease negotiations.

So far as cables installed by tenants for their use during the term, tenants should expect that landlords will require those tenants to remove the cables they are abandoning at the end of the lease term.

Whether abandoned cables are to be removed by landlords or tenants, it will involve a considerable expense, but one that is necessary for health and safety.

Exterior Communications Equipment

Many tenants require the right to mount communications equipment, such as antennas, dishes, or other items (whether they now exist or may exist in the future) on the exterior of the building in which the premises are situated. Landlords are generally willing to accommodate those tenant's requirements, subject of course, to certain protections.

Landlords are, of course, concerned that all applicable laws and other governmental requirements are met. Those requirements include those pertaining to zoning, aviation limitations, appearance requirements, and such other requirements as governmental bodies may, in their wisdom, impose.

Lease Provisions Specific to Certain Types of Leases | 5

Earlier in this book, I touched on some of the issues to be discussed below. Although I have given you, the reader, a foretaste of those issues, I feel that to properly inform you, it is appropriate to discuss them in greater detail. For example, although I just discussed matters relating to rent, I am dealing with it again because certain items that make up "rent," other than those discussed above, tend to be specific to certain types of leases. Thus, percentage rent is specific to retail leasing, as is the payment of certain common area expenses. Industrial/warehouse and office leases may also provide for the payment of common area expenses, but office leases customarily provide for the payment of operating expenses instead. These are all "pass-throughs" and are deemed to be "rent" for the reasons expressed on page 115. Anyway, a little review is not a bad thing.

Percentage Rent

I discussed percentage rent briefly on page 17. To reiterate, percentage rent is rent calculated based on the sales from retail premises. Of course, not all retail leases provide for percentage rent; many have other means of protecting the landlord from inflation. Some have specified amounts or a percentage increase in the stated rent, either annually or at other times, or upon the exercise of an option to extend or expand; and some provide for those financial escalations and also for percentage rent. For example, a lease might provide for a fixed minimum rent of $60,000 per year for the first year, $61,800 for the second year (being a 3% increase), and so on, and still require the tenant to pay percentage rent. That usually occurs when the percentage rent breakpoint is so high that the landlord does not really expect to collect percentage rent unless the tenant does exceptionally well or inflation is very high.

So how does percentage rent work? Let's assume a lease to a clothing store in which the percentage rent is the only financial escalation, that the annual stated rent is $50,000, and that the agreed percentage is 5%. Is the tenant paying 5% of all sales, or just sales above an agreed "break point"? In our lease, the "natural" break point is $1 million. How is that determined? In the absence of a stated rent, when the tenant has sold $1 million of goods and services, it will be obligated to pay $50,000 in percentage rent. However, the stated rent is a minimum rent, which is to be paid whether the tenant sells $1,000 or $1 million, so the parties agree that if the tenant sells more than $1 million, it must pay additional rent of the excess based on the 5% agreed to.

Of course, the percentage to be paid by tenants will vary from deal to deal, and some types of retailers pay more and some pay less. Drug stores and supermarkets tend to pay less percentage rent, if any, while tenants who sell at substantial mark-ups tend to pay more.

Nor is it unusual for a lease to provide that the tenant is to pay a stated percentage on all its sales and provide for a deduction for the stated rent. Also, the percentage may vary depending on the volume of sales, sometimes increasing and sometimes decreasing. Thus, a lease might provide as follows: "Tenant shall pay, as percentage rent, 5% of gross sales until gross sales exceed $1 million, and 5% of gross sales in excess of $1 million until gross sales exceed $2 million, and 7% of gross sales in excess of $2 million. Tenant shall be entitled to a credit against percentage rent in an amount equal to the fixed minimum rent paid by Tenant." Note that, as drafted, if the fixed minimum rent is abated during a part of a year (such as by reason of a fire), but the tenant's sales are excellent during the balance of the year, the landlord still gets the full rent (it could accomplish the same thing by adjusting the break point, but that is not as sneaky).

When is percentage rent paid? The tenant prefers that it be paid at the end of the year, preferably the calendar year after the Christmas season. The landlord will want it paid in monthly installments, with an adjustment at the end of each lease year—for three reasons. First, it wants the use of the money. Second, it may be concerned about the credit of the tenant. And third, if the lease starts in the middle of the year, it will receive a bump in the payment right after the Christmas season and the downward adjustment may not occur until the following June, giving the landlord the use of more of the tenant's money.

Percentage rent is usually paid based on the tenant's gross sales as defined in the lease. Typically, *gross sales* means the gross amount charged for all sales made or services rendered on or from the premises, including sales made by licensees or concessionaires. Each sale is valued at the actual sales price charged the customer and reported in full in the month in which the sale occurs, even if the sale is a credit or installment sale or if full payment is not received at the time of the sale, and even if the goods are not delivered until a later date.

Usually, the tenant negotiates for exclusions from gross sales, some of which are not controversial, but others generate a lot of discussion. Some of the non-controversial exclusions may even be included in the landlord's lease form. The landlord usually agrees to exclude sales taxes, returned goods, goods transferred to tenant's other stores where the transfer is not for the purpose of consummating a sale, and sales out of the ordinary course of business, such as sales in bulk. Sometimes the landlord will agree to exclude sales to employees at cost or at a substantial discount. Landlords will balk at excluding charges made by credit card companies, as that is simply a cost of doing business, but if a merchant extends credit itself, exclusion for bad debts may be agreed to, subject to a maximum percentage of sales.

If a tenant has more than one store and the sale occurs in the other store and the goods are delivered from the premises, percentage rent should not be payable in both places, but the parties will have to decide which landlord gets the credit for the sale. If goods are purchased at another store but returned at this one, which store gets to deduct the sale? If goods are sold on the Internet but delivered from the premises, percentage rent is often charged, and it might also be charged if the item is ordered online at the premises but delivered directly to the customer's home. There is also an issue regarding gift certificates. Are they included when and where they are sold or when and where they are redeemed? What if they are sold at another store and redeemed at this one or vice versa?

As can be seen, just finalizing the definition of *gross sales* can be very difficult and time-consuming, but then we move on to the issue of record keeping. What good is agreeing to the definition of *gross sales* if there is no foolproof way to ensure that all sales are properly recorded? The lease form might specify some method of recording sales, but in the negotiations the tenant announces that it customarily uses another method and changing its methods can be extremely expensive; further, the tenant does not want to have different methods for different stores.

So how does the tenant's method ensure that the proper amount of percentage rent will be paid? Certainly, the tenant has a strong interest in knowing how the store is doing, but that does not mean that it is averse to hiding the facts from the landlord (and perhaps the sales tax authorities). In small restaurants, where checks are paid to a cashier, often in cash, many sales may not be recorded at all. And once the parties agree on the method of record keeping, the lease will also provide the landlord the right to audit the tenant's records to make certain that it is not being cheated, with penalties built in for underpayment.

Providing for percentage rent builds an entirely new administrative hassle into rent payment, so it is no wonder that many landlords try to avoid percentage rent and to rely on other methods of financial escalation to protect their profits. That does not mean, however, that percentage rent will go away.

Pass-Throughs

Pass-throughs consist of all the expenses customarily incurred by the landlord for which the tenant is liable under the lease, either by paying the expense directly or by reimbursing the landlord for expenses paid by the landlord. Pass-throughs differ from one type of lease to another, and also differ depending on the leasing situation in each type of lease.

Ground Leases

In situations where the tenant leases a piece of ground from the landlord and builds its own building, the tenant generally owns title to the building, at least for the term of the lease, but whether it owns it or not, the tenant typically pays all of the costs of maintaining and insuring the building, and to restore the building after a casualty loss. The lease will also require the tenant to pay all the real estate taxes pertaining to the land and building.

Single-Tenant Leases

Similarly, if the tenant leases an industrial/warehouse building or a big box retail store, or any free standing building in which it is the only tenant, the lease—particularly if it is a long-term lease—may provide that the tenant undertake all of the same responsibilities. These are true "triple net" leases with the tenant paying the taxes; property and liability insurance; and maintenance, repairs, and replacements. These leases were sometimes called "net and bond" leases because of their similarity to coupon bonds. The landlord does nothing other than to collect the rent, pay the debt service if there is a mortgage, and keep the balance of the proceeds. This is the least complex situation for the landlord, but let us add some complexity.

Assume that the building is somewhat old and may, during the course of the lease, need a new roof. The roof-top HVAC unit is old and may need replacement during the term. The parking lot may need resurfacing. The tenant is willing to pay for repairs and maintenance, but not for replacements. Further, it is not willing to pay for structural problems that may result because of the age of the building. Here is where you get into some negotiation.

Perhaps the landlord is willing to pay to replace the roof, the HVAC equipment, or the parking lot, provided the tenant has diligently inspected and repaired it as long as it can be made useful. However, if the lease term is long enough or the tenant has options to extend, or even if it extends the lease by amendment, the landlord will want the tenant to be obligated to pay for subsequent replacements on the theory that the tenant has used up the useful life of the replaced item. An alternative is to provide that the tenant will pay for the replacement over time, based on the useful life of the replaced item, plus some interest factor to reimburse the landlord for having advanced the cost of the replacement. Of course, the tenant will not want to pay any of it.

As to problems with the structure, landlords tend to refuse to take on the responsibility on the theory that the building is old, and the tenant is paying a rental based on an old building. Problems that arise are most likely not caused by defects in the original construction. The risk is minimal (although I have represented clients in situations where structural walls started bowing out), so if the tenant is afforded the opportunity to do an inspection, it is likely to accept the landlord's position.

Some net leases provide that the tenant is to carry the property insurance and be obligated to rebuild the premises after a loss. There are issues here, too. If the tenant carries the property insurance, it should also be required to carry the business income insurance to provide proceeds for the payment of the rent, since it is cheaper to carry business income insurance along with the property insurance than to carry it separately. If that is the case, the lease should not provide for rent abatement since the tenant, and not the landlord, will have the insurance proceeds applicable to the rents (and the business income insurance should cover all rent [including taxes], and not just the base rent). An interesting side issue is that most leases drafted in this manner do not deal with the situation where there is an uninsured casualty, such as earthquake or flood.[1] The tenant's obligation to rebuild under those circumstances may come as quite a surprise to it.

There might also be rail service that serves more than one property with a single rail spur. Any maintenance costs imposed by the railroad will have to be properly allocated among the rail users only, so that if there are three buildings in the complex that could use the rail service, but only two use it, those costs will have to be allocated to them, either by usage or by square footage of the served building.

---

1. Although earthquake and flood insurance are available in earthquake or flood hazard areas, they are not available in areas of minimal risk, even though such losses are possible there as well. Further, earthquake insurance, where available, is very expensive, and the coverage may not be sufficient to repair a major loss.

Multi-Tenant Industrial/Warehouse Leases

Moving up in complexity, we have the multi-tenant industrial/warehouse leases—anything from a two-tenant building, each with direct access to the parking areas and its own truck docks, to those with numerous tenants, sometimes with common corridors and common truck docks. Certainly, the landlord will have to be more involved in the operation of this type of project.

The landlord and not the tenants will be paying the taxes, carrying the property insurance (and also liability and other insurance), and performing maintenance, repairs, and replacements (except for interior ones and for damage caused by the tenant). Further, the landlord and not the tenant will be contesting tax assessments, and that will involve costs that the landlord will seek to pass on to the tenant. In addition, the landlord has to perform the management function or hire an outside manager. The landlord will look to the tenants to pay their respective share of all those costs, either on a "net lease" basis or as part of their gross rent, but with stops. Thus, these leases typically require tenants to pay their pro rata share (sometimes referred to as proportionate share) of taxes, the landlord's insurance, and also the maintenance expenses and assessments imposed by the association that maintains the common areas of the business park containing the building within which the premises are located.

Stops are discussed in some detail above (see page 12), but to reiterate, stops are the amount in a gross lease over which the tenant pays its share of the applicable expense. Theoretically, the base rent includes a factor for taxes and common area (or operating) expenses, which include insurance and maintenance, payable for the year in which the base rent is determined (which may be the first year of the term or the immediately prior year, or even the year following, if the pass-throughs do not begin until the year after that); so the hedge against inflation consists of the tenant's paying for those expenses to the extent that they exceed the amount for that base year.

Sometimes the base amount is a specified amount, such as $3 per square foot for taxes, $.50 per square foot for common area (or operating) expenses, or the amount might be specified as the square footage amounts multiplied by the *total* square footage—each is a specified or calculable number. That is fine if the specified amounts represent the actual or realistically anticipated costs, but if the specified amounts are less than the actual or anticipated costs, the tenant will be overpaying *every year during the entire term* by the amount of the difference. Thus, it is imperative that the tenant's lawyer determine what the actual or anticipated costs will be.

Some leases state that tenant will pay its pro rata share of the excess over a particular year, such as "taxes in excess of the taxes assessed against the property [or payable] for the year 2013" and "maintenance costs in excess of those paid or incurred by Landlord in the year 2013. There are things to be considered in that situation, too. What if the taxes for 2013 were not fully assessed because the building on the property is new or because the owner got relief due to economic hardship? In that situation, the tenant will be overcharged for taxes fully assessed in each of the subsequent years during the entire term. Likewise, if maintenance costs were reduced because the building or the equipment was under a warranty that provided for free repairs for a year, or the expenses were not for a fully occupied building, and that reduction was reflected in the base, the tenant would again be overcharged in subsequent years.

Some of the same issues apply in multi-tenant situations as applied in the single-tenant situation. What if the landlord incurs expenses for roof replacement or other "capital expenses"? Are the tenants to be billed some share of those costs? If so, should the costs be amortized, and over what period and with what interest factor? Here is a zinger—what if there are several buildings in the complex with common parking areas but obviously separate roofs? Should the tenants in Building B be required to pay for the replacement, or even just the repair, of the roof of Building A, especially if Building A is 10 years older than Building B?

That brings us to another complicated issue—the definition of *pro rata share*. Pro rata share is usually defined as a percentage calculated by dividing the rentable area of the premises by the total rentable area of the building (or the property), and that works in most situations. However, take the situation where there are two equally sized spaces, one of which is a warehouse with one small, dinky office (Tenant 1) and the other (Tenant 2) is 25% warehouse and 75% fancy, executive offices. Let's assume that the tax assessor in that jurisdiction is efficient and will discover the difference by inspecting the property or even just by looking at the building permits—it is not a secret. Is it fair to charge Tenant 1 50% of the total tax? A better question is: Is it appropriate to charge Tenant 2 only 50% of the tax? The answer to both questions is "no."

Here is what frequently happens: The landlord charges 50% of the tax to Tenant 1 and charges 75% of the tax to Tenant 2. This is known as "double dipping." Is it fair? Is it right? Of course not. Does it occur? Certainly. The lawyer representing Tenant 1 has a duty to try to protect its client from the old double dip, but it is not easy—he or she must first be aware of the risk. It is even more difficult to protect Tenant 1 if it leases the property before Tenant 2 comes into the picture, or perhaps when the Tenant 2 space is still leased to a company with its own small, dinky office.

In a multi-building complex, there might be separate pro rata shares for separate expenses, so that taxes, insurance, and parking lot maintenance may be one pro rata share, but roof replacement and other building maintenance expenses may be shared on a different basis. In a multi-use building, there may be a prorata share for taxes and expenses allowable to the entire building, and for operating expenses applicable only to a portion.

One more word about pro rata shares: Some leases will define *pro rata share* in terms of "leased and occupied area" rather than "rentable area." This is terribly unfair to tenants because it requires the existing tenants to pay the expenses for unleased space. There is an issue here for landlords. How is the landlord going to recoup expenses paid only for leased spaces? That can be handled by grossing up, as will be discussed under "Office Leases" below.

Office Leases

If you think that multi-tenant industrial/warehouse lease pass-throughs are complex, follow me as I move on to office leases, which typically provide for the payment, on a net basis, or as a payment of costs in excess of a stop, of taxes and operating expenses. As to taxes, the issues are similar to those in multi-tenant industrial/warehouse leases, which are discussed above. As to operating expenses, however, we are in an entirely new ballgame—a most expansive list of items for which the landlord charges the tenants. I will digress from my usual practice of not including lease language by quoting, at length, the definition of operating expenses in an actual lease form. Then

I will discuss the problems that I would raise if I were representing a tenant and encountered this language:

'Operating Expenses' means all expenses, paid or incurred on behalf of the Landlord in respect of the ownership, management, operation, and maintenance of the Property which, in accordance with generally accepted accounting principles as applied to the operation of first class office building properties, are properly chargeable to the ownership, management, operation, and maintenance of the Property including, without limitation, employees (including the amount of any social security taxes, unemployment insurance contributions, and "fringe benefits"), insurance premiums, fuel costs and utility costs, property owners association assessments, management fees and repairs to the Property, replacements of Property and Building components (except footings, floor slabs, exterior walls, columns, and structural portions of the roof) amortized on a straight line basis over the useful life of the replaced component (which useful life shall be reasonably determined by the contractor replacing the same). Operating Expenses shall also specifically include the costs, as reasonably amortized by Landlord with interest at the rate of 18% per annum on the unamortized amount, of any capital improvement which reduces other Operating Expenses, but only in an amount not to exceed in any one year the reduction of such expense for that year. Operating Expenses shall not include: (1) any interest expense on mortgages placed upon the Property; (2) franchise or income taxes imposed upon Landlord; (3) the cost of any work or service performed in any instance for any tenant (including the Tenant) at the cost of such tenant; (4) expenses incurred by Landlord as a result of a fire or other casualty or as a result of a taking by way of eminent domain; (5) expenses incurred in leasing or procuring new tenants; (6) legal expenses in enforcing the terms of any leases; or (7) wages, salaries, or other compensation paid to any executive employee above the grade of building superintendent. If the Building is not fully occupied during any Year, the variable Operating Expenses for that year shall be equitably adjusted as though the Building were fully occupied. Further, if Landlord is not furnishing any particular work or service (the cost of which if performed by Landlord would constitute an Operating Expense) to a tenant who had undertaken to perform such work or service in lieu of its performance by Landlord, Operating Expenses shall be deemed for the purposes of this Section to be increased by an amount equal to the additional Operating Expenses which would reasonably have been incurred by Landlord if it had at its own expense furnished such work or service to such tenant.

Sorry about that (although you lawyers should be used to reading stuff like that), but now let's pick it apart.

Note that there is language as to what is included generally, and then there are examples of the things that are included. Next there are exclusions, and finally there are some provisions for what is referred to as "grossing up."

The general inclusion language has two problems. First, it includes "ownership" expenses. Those are not listed in the examples, but some are, in fact, listed among the exclusions, as items 1, 2, 5, 6 and 7. Why, however, should *any* ownership expenses be paid by the tenants? Should the tenants have to pay for the ownership entity's accountant in preparing its financial statements or tax returns? More importantly, should it have to pay interest on non-mortgage loans or principal on any loans at all? Ownership expenses should not be passed on to tenants—period!

The second problem with the general inclusion language is that it states that generally accepted accounting principles (GAAP) should be used to determine what is properly applied to the ownership, management, operation, and maintenance of the property. I am not an accountant and thus not very familiar with GAAP, but it seems to me that a better standard than GAAP would be "reasonable management practices" or words to that effect.

Now we have a series of examples. Note that they are examples only. Other items that may fall within the general inclusion language are not excluded unless they are listed in the exclusion section. The example that pops out is the reference to management. This is a blank check for the landlord. There is no limit on what the landlord may charge for management, whether it does the management itself or contracts with an outside manager (the boss's proverbial brother-in-law?). The management fee should be capped, either here or in additional exclusions, which I will discuss below.

The next items relate to capital expenditures—not defined here, but often limited to what must be depreciated rather than expensed under applicable tax laws. This language requires the tenant to pay capital expenditures, amortized over their useful life, as determined by the contractor doing the work (some leases provide for a much faster amortization). Tenants might object to paying for any capital items at all, and this is an area for negotiation. The language specifically provides for amortization of cost-cutting capital expenditures (albeit at an unreasonably high rate of interest), but only to the extent of the savings. Here the language is more generous to tenants than you may see in other leases, which do not have such a limitation.

Let us skip the exclusions for the moment, as they will be discussed below. Suffice it to say that they are inadequate. We will move on to grossing up. Strangely, this language is not unfair to tenants, although many tenants (and their lawyers) do not wholly understand the concept and think it is a blank check for landlords to double dip. I often use the following example in explaining this language:

An office building has 20,000 square feet of rentable area. Half of the building is leased to an office tenant, and the other half is vacant. The pro rata share of the tenant with the leased space is 50%. Only the leased space is cleaned by the landlord's janitor service, which costs $1 per square foot per year. The janitor service is, to the landlord, an expense that varies with the level of occupancy of the property. Without the grossing up language in the lease, the tenant occupying 10,000 square feet would pay 50% of the $10,000 cost for the service, or $5,000, even though the cost of cleaning its own space is actually $10,000. It is a windfall for the tenant, and the landlord has to pay the balance even though it gets no benefit from the cleaning. The same principle applies even if the other space is leased, but to a business such as a bank, which does its own cleaning because of its security concerns.

Now let us move on to exclusions. I have my own list of exclusions, which I will share with you. Some of them cover the same ground as items 1–7 in the language above, but here they are:

1. the cost to Landlord of any work or services performed in any instances for any tenant (including Tenant) at the cost of such tenant;

2. capital expenses (except for costs of any capital improvements made or installed for the purpose of reducing Operating Expenses (and then only to the extent of such reduction in expenses) or made or installed pursuant to governmental law enacted after the date hereof, which shall be amortized in accordance with Generally Accepted Accounting Principles consistently applied);

3. wages, salaries, and other benefits for staff above the level of building manager;

4. any expense or costs associated with bringing the Property into compliance with any law, ordinance, or code in effect as of the date of this Lease;

5. cost of any service furnished to any other occupant of the Property which Landlord does not provide to Tenant hereunder;

6. penalties, fines, or interest due to violations of contracts, laws, rules, or regulations or due to late payments of taxes, utility bills, or other contractual obligations;

7. costs of environmental remediation;

8. costs of repairs due to the negligence or intentional misconduct of Landlord or its employees, agents, or contractors;

9. advertising, space planning expenses, legal fees, brokerage commissions, tenant improvements, allowances, concessions, and other expenses incurred in procuring tenants for the Property;

10. legal fees, court costs, or other fees or costs of enforcing leases;

11. any costs for which Landlord is reimbursed (whether by insurance or otherwise);

12. cost of repairs, alterations, or replacements caused by casualty losses or other events to the extent actually insured or self-insured against by Landlord or required to be insured against by Landlord pursuant to this Lease;

13. cost of repairs, alterations, or replacements caused by the exercise of rights of condemnation or eminent domain;

14. fees or other compensation paid to subsidiaries or affiliates of Landlord for services on or to the Property, to the extent that the costs of such services exceed competitive costs of such services;

15. repairs or replacements of any equipment or component of the Property caused by deficient design, selection of materials, construction, or improper maintenance;

16. costs relating to maintaining Landlord's existence, either as a corporation, partnership, or other entity, such as trustee's fees, annual fees, partnership organization or administration expenses, business, corporation or franchise taxes, deed recordation expenses, legal and accounting fees;

17. costs for purchasing and installing sculpture, paintings, or other objects of art; and

18. management fees in excess of 3% of gross receipts from the Property.

Note that capital expenditures are totally excluded in this list. Expect a negotiation on that one.

Special consideration has to be given to the multi-purpose office building—a building or complex with retail and office premises, or even residential units. While the language in the leases pertaining to those respective uses might parallel that in leases for a building with only one use, when it comes to pass-throughs there are special problems to address. Does the assessor assess different uses at different valuations? If so, how is the tax portion of the pass-throughs to be allocated between the portions of the property? Retailers generally clean their own space, so how are the operating expenses allocable to janitor service to be handled? Are there more common areas for the retail space? Are there restaurants causing greater cleanup requirements in the common areas? How are parking requirements increased, and how are the additional costs for maintenance and snow removal to be dealt with? How can tenants avoid double dipping by the landlord in such a complex situation? How can these issues be dealt with directly and with a minimum of special lease provisions? I cannot really attempt to answer these questions because the situations are so diverse, but it is certainly important to raise the issues.

Retail Leases

Retail leases customarily include the same types of tax provisions as are included in industrial/warehouse leases and in office leases. They might also include operating expenses language (or comparable common area maintenance expense language) such as was discussed in the office lease section above. That language may partake of the same issues and must be carefully reviewed.

In the situation where there is a free-standing store in an urban setting with no common areas, the landlord may not be providing any services; the tenant may even be required to do snow removal from the sidewalk in front of the store. In that situation, there will be no operating expense or common area pass-throughs. At the other extreme is the enclosed regional mall with very extensive services rendered by the landlord. Most retail is somewhere between the two.

In the enclosed mall situation, the landlord has a great variety of expenses to pass through to the tenants. The enclosure itself is a vast common area. There is heating and cooling of the enclosed common areas in addition to heating and cooling the various store premises. There may be roof leaks in the enclosed common area and other special maintenance problems. If some of the stores open on the enclosed mall and some do not, allocation of the pro rata share for each type of tenant could present problems because the mall stores will be paying for heating and cooling the mall itself, for extra security, and for extensive cleaning and maintenance. The tenant's lawyer must confirm that the costs are properly allocated.

Shopping malls, whether enclosed or not, have many common area costs. If it is in the North, there is snow and ice removal. There is landscape maintenance, North or South. There is certainly security. There are cleaning crews. Of course, there are costs for general maintenance, repairs, and replacements. Landlords will seek to pass those costs through to the tenants so as to maintain the contemplated net return on their investments. As in other types of properties, tenants will be concerned about quantifying their risks and reducing surprise expenses. They will want to confirm that, in a gross lease with stops, the stops provided for in the lease are really the base expenses, as discussed above.

There may also be outlots on the shopping mall property that participate in some of the expenses and not others.[2] For example, if there is a parking lot shared by the mall and the outlots, how are those costs to be allocated? What if one of the outlot tenants is a movie theater that has parking requirements that are especially large, considering the number of theater seats? The theater has extended hours. The outlot tenant may be a restaurant that has extended hours as well, or it may be a fast-food facility that generates a lot of debris in the parking lot.

Obviously, the pro rata share of various tenants may depend on a number of considerations. There is a serious one that may arise in the case of a mall or shopping center with a major tenant, such as a department store, a major discounter, or a big-box operator. That tenant may negotiate a deal under which its contribution to operating expenses or common area expenses is capped at a level far below what it would be if it were paying its straight, pro rata share of those expenses. The rationale is that, since the major tenant creates considerable traffic for the mall or center, the other tenants derive a special benefit from that tenant's being there and, in effect, should subsidize that tenant. It is probable that a more accurate statement of the reason that a major tenant requests that benefit is that it has the economic clout to get it. In either case, giving such a concession to a major tenant means that all the other tenants' pro rata shares are increased so that they are not really in proportion to the rentable area of the property.

As you can see, the base or fixed minimum rent negotiated by the parties (or their brokers) is the tip of the iceberg. It is additional rent, either in the form of financial escalations or pass-throughs, that may determine the real economics of the lease, and as to those, the "devil is in the details."

---

2. An outlot is an area on the periphery of the landlord's property that is not, technically, part of the shopping mall and that is leased or held for lease by a restaurant, a bank, or a similar tenant that needs parking and ready access to the adjoining streets. It may be owned by an unrelated party. Allocation of the various expenses may be governed by a Declaration of Easements, Covenants and Restrictions that will, among other things, allocate costs among the parties.

Relocation

Another possible issue, particularly in office leases (although it may also occur in retail or industrial/warehouse leases but not with the same frequency), is the right of the landlord to relocate the tenant to other premises. Landlords want this right to deal with situations in which the location of an existing tenant might prevent the landlord from leasing a substantial amount of space to another tenant. For example, because other tenants have vacated, a small tenant might be the only tenant on a large floor. If the landlord has the possibility to lease the entire floor to a new tenant, it will want to relocate the small tenant to another floor in the building, or even to other space in a nearby building owned by the landlord or by an entity related to the landlord. In a retail situation, a new tenant may require certain frontage, which may require the landlord to relocate an existing tenant into adjoining space on the other side, or even to a new location in the mall. The landlord is usually willing, under those circumstances, to pay for the move, even one that is very expensive, if the landlord determines that there will be a substantial net economic benefit to it.

Relocation is very problematic for tenants, even if the landlord agrees to relocate the tenant over a weekend, is willing to pay all the costs, and to minimize the inconvenience to the tenant. The first issue for the tenant is the description of the replacement premises. If the tenant leased its space because it had certain views or was on an upper floor of a multi-story building, it would want the new space to have comparable view or not be on a lower floor. In the retail mall situation, the tenant may have selected its location because of traffic generated by certain other tenants, and that tenant will be very fussy as to the location of the new premises.[3]

Usually, lease provisions dealing with relocation state that the replacement space will be approximately the same size, but are vague on the amount of the variation. If the space is 10% smaller, it may not work for the tenant.

---

3. Moving a retail tenant that has already fixtured its store is usually even more expensive than relocating an office tenant.

If it is smaller at all, the rent (and pro rata share) should be reduced. If it is larger, the tenant does not want to pay more rent or additional rent.

An issue rarely considered in the landlord's lease is the configuration of the space. Just because a space is the same size does not mean that it will work for the tenant. It might be too long and narrow, or have a vast open area and too little window access. In short, the tenant will want the space to truly be comparable.

Finally, there is the issue of what costs will actually be borne by the landlord. The tenant will want the landlord to build out the new space to look like the old one, including decoration and amenities; it will want the landlord to install cabling for all its phones and computer equipment; it will want the furniture, fixtures, equipment, and all of the tenant's other personal property to be moved by a responsible mover that will put the new premises in condition for immediate use. The tenant will also insist that the landlord pay for replacement of stationary and other printed materials that had identified the old location.

Relocation does not actually occur very often because it is very expensive for landlords. However, it does occur occasionally and the tenant is really entitled to have its operation protected to the maximum extent possible.

Measuring the Premises

I have made numerous references to *rentable area*. but I have not defined it. It would seem that the definition should be simple, but it isn't.

First let me define *usable area*, which is the area in the premises that is actually usable by the tenant for the operation of its business. It may include the warehouse and office, in the case of a multi-tenant industrial/warehouse lease; the sales, office, and storage area in a retail lease; and, in the office lease, the offices themselves, employee lounges, reception areas, and other internal areas used only by the tenant and its employees. It is basically the areas that are for the tenants' exclusive use.

The problem arises from the fact that almost all multi-tenant buildings have common areas—areas in the building that are used by more than one tenant and the employees, guests, or customers of those tenants, as well as areas used by the landlord to service the tenants. Typical common areas in an office building, for example, are the lobby, common corridors, restrooms, janitor closets, mechanical and electrical areas, and even the exterior walls of the structure. Since those facilities are for the benefit of all of the tenants, most leases provide that a share of those common areas is, in effect, leased to the tenants. Accordingly, the tenants pay for their usable space plus their share of the common areas, and the total is the tenants' "rentable area." In fact, the area of the entire building that is being divided among the tenants, excepting only vertical penetrations in a multi-floor building (such as staircases and elevator shafts) is included in the "rentable area." The difference between the rentable area and the usable area of a building is now referred to as the "loss factor."

Obviously, in the single tenant situation, the rentable area is the whole building, but even there issues may arise. Assume, for example, that you are representing the landlord in a small, urban, single-tenant retail building fronting directly on a commercial street. The structure is designed so that part of the façade is set back from the property line. In that situation, the landlord may wish to make the property line the boundary for the premises and include the setback area in rentable area.

Usually leases merely specify the tenant's rentable area and its pro rata share of taxes and common area expenses, and tenants just accept that. However, sophisticated tenants, especially in buildings with large loss factors, sometimes question that or even contest the measurement of their usable area and also how the rentable area has been calculated.

Rentable area issues can arise in all multi-tenant leasing situations, but I will focus on offices leases as an example.

Office Leases

Let's say you represent a tenant in a 10 story, 300,000-square-foot, multi-tenant building that has a loss factor of 4%—that is, 4% of the building is common area (except that it is now referred to in the BOMA standards [discussed below] as the "service and amenity area" to differentiate between traditional common areas and non-traditional amenities such as conference rooms provided free to tenants, but I will continue to call them common areas). Your client is leasing the top five floors—half the building.

All the corridors will be internal, as will the restrooms and other facilities that are usually common areas. In fact, the only common areas being used by your client will be the building lobby. Shouldn't your client's rentable area be equal to its usable area, with an add-on only for the lobby? If its share of the 4% is added to its rent, it is seriously overpaying.

On the other hand, let's assume that you represent a tenant on a multi-tenant floor in the lower five stories of the same building, and let's assume that the five-floor tenant did not negotiate the exclusion of what would otherwise have been common areas on its floors. However, the actual loss factor is not 4%; it is really 2%, plus the lobby (but let us leave that aside for the purpose of this discussion). Under those circumstances, that smaller tenant is overpaying instead.

If you are not familiar with the BOMA measurement standards, perhaps you should be. While it is certainly possible for the parties to a lease to define binding measurement standards for that lease, generally the parties refer to the standards created by Building Owners and Managers Association International (BOMA)—often without knowing what those standards are. BOMA has developed standards not only for office buildings but also for industrial and retail buildings and for residential multi-tenant buildings.

BOMA released a standard for multi-use buildings in June 2011. The standards are contained in five books. They are very complicated and are frequently revised. I admit that I am not an expert in those standards, but even if I were, this is not the place for an extended discussion. The standards can be purchased from BOMA, and BOMA even has "Official Interpreters" to assist its purchasers in understanding those standards. If you have serious measurement issues, either in connection with representing landlords or tenants, or even if you feel it appropriate to be familiar with them, you can buy the standards. As of this writing, the BOMA website for the purchase of the standards is http://www.store.boma.org. It may, however, be easier simply to consult an architect and let him or her try to figure them out.

Covenants

By covenants, I mean agreements in the lease whereby the tenant or the landlord agrees to perform or refrain from performing certain acts that impact the property or the economics of the property for the other party. Many covenants have already been discussed in the section of this book entitled "Lease Provisions Common to Most Leases." However, there are some covenants that are peculiar to particular leases, which I would like to discuss here.

Covenants in Industrial/Warehouse Leases

A key covenant in many of these leases is the obligation to operate the business only for the permitted use or purpose and for no other purposes. A careful landlord will evaluate the use and nature of the use of its tenants to make certain that the tenant will not cause unexpected damage to the premises. The landlord may even visit the tenant's prior premises to see how it operates and to make certain that the premises are suitable for the tenant's use, so that the tenant will not be asking to make alterations that would make the premises less leasable after the term expires.

Landlords, not surprisingly, are very concerned that the tenant's operations could create an environmental law violation or, more stringently, that the tenant may be using hazardous substances (the tenant, on the other hand, wants to make certain that the premises do not have pre-existing conditions that might create a problem for it). The landlord may be concerned about trucks on the parking lot, which may be designed for the weight of automobiles but not for trucks. It may want to know how trucks will be staged when delivering or picking up goods, whether they might be blocking the roads, or standing with their motors running for long periods of time. The lease may prohibit outside storage or, if it is allowed, require fencing or screening. Once the landlord has a good understanding of the tenant's business, it can insert language in its lease to protect itself, such as it tried to do in the stinky fish case I discussed on page ___. Food handling or processing is an especially potent area for covenants, because of the possible need for refrigeration, the risk of vermin infestation, and issues of garbage handling and odors.

From the tenant's perspective, the tenant and its lawyer should examine the covenants in the lease to confirm that they do not actually prevent the tenant from using the premises to conduct its intended business. The space may simply not be suitable for the tenant.

Covenants in Office Leases

Here again we must take into account the type of office lease we are considering. One of the problems with writing a book of this kind is that both the writer and the reader tend to view a category of leases as something monolithic. Say *office* and we may think of a downtown or suburban office building and not of the one-story building, perhaps with a single tenant. Keeping in mind that you may also have to review and negotiate leases for those smaller buildings, however, this discussion will proceed on the assumption that we are dealing with a multi-story office building either in the central business district or in an outlying area (the major difference between the two being the availability of on-site parking).

It is difficult to cover all the covenants binding on tenants since the entire lease creates such obligations. For example, tenants are required to comply with applicable laws and ordinances and the requirements of the landlord's insurance underwriters. Tenants may not bring hazardous materials on the premises. Some of those covenants are particularly acute in medical office buildings, where tenants may be doing x-rays or treating patients with substances that should be safeguarded and not permitted to go into the drains or the atmosphere. Medical office leases tend to have more restrictions than general office leases.

Many of the covenants binding on tenants are those that sometimes find their way into rules and regulations attached as exhibits to leases. Typically, they deal with subjects like prohibiting animals (except service animals), not defacing elevators, closing the corridor door, lettering on entranceways, not raising the landlord's insurance costs, or keeping dangerous materials on the premises. I like to include those provisions in the lease itself rather than in separate rules and regulations (although my lease form permits the landlord to make rules and regulations in the future). Sometimes, however, landlords want many and very specific provisions, and in that case, the exhibit format may be more appropriate. In fact, I once reviewed an office lease that had 38 general rules and 11 parking rules (plus 43 rules for contractors attached to the workletter). That, in my judgment, was overkill.

Tenants (and lawyers) often ignore a rules and regulations exhibit. That could be a dangerous mistake. The lease probably states that violation of rules and regulations is a default under the lease. That means that those rules and regulations are an integral part of the lease even if they are hidden in the back. There may be rules that are inconsistent with other provisions in the lease—other provisions for which you have negotiated. That creates an ambiguity. They may impose additional obligations on the tenant that were not contemplated by it and that, if they had been in the body of the lease, would have been negotiated out. Treating rules and regulations to be meaningless boilerplate is a very bad idea.

Office leases also impose or should impose obligations on the landlord that are extremely important to the tenant—the obligation to provide services. Here is a typical list of services from a lease form I use:

1. Maintenance of the exterior and all structural parts of the Building, the common areas and the parking areas, and the plumbing, sewage and drainage systems (except the plumbing, sewage and drainage systems serving the Premises only).
2. Heat and air conditioning of common areas, during normal business hours, Saturdays, Sundays and holidays excepted, whenever heat or air conditioning shall, in Landlord's judgment, be required to maintain comfortable temperature and humidity.
3. Lighting of common areas and parking areas during appropriate hours, depending upon seasons of the year.
4. Snow plowing in parking and exterior common areas.
5. Maintenance of landscaping in the common areas.
6. Window washing of the exterior of all windows in the Premises and the Building, weather permitting, at intervals to be determined by the Landlord.
7. All janitorial and cleanup services (including rubbish removal).
8. Maintenance of all heating, ventilating and air conditioning equipment installed by the Landlord.
9. Water for drinking, lavatory and toilet purposes.

10. Elevator service (which may be reduced during non-business hours or to service the elevators, provided that some service will be available at all times).

It is a nice list, but both lawyers should be aware of the issues it raises. In 2, what are the "normal business hours"? Normal for whom? What heat and air conditioning will be provided "after hours" to accountants during the tax season? What is the charge for after-hours HVAC? How much notice will the landlord require to provide after-hours HVAC? Just what temperature will be maintained during the various seasons of the year? What holidays justify turning down the heat; can the landlord do so on Columbus Day, for example?

As to 6, how often will the exterior windows be washed? Regarding 7, just what are the standards for the janitorial services and what is the frequency? If the landlord has a contract for those services that specifies what is to be done and where, it should be attached as an exhibit as specifying what the landlord will provide subject, perhaps, to minor modifications.

Obviously, all the services are important to the tenant, but some may be more important than others since, without them, the tenant is unable to operate its business. It can live without janitor service for a week if there is a strike, but it cannot live without elevator service if it is on the 42nd floor.

So what happens if vital services are interrupted? There are two situations here: one in which it is outside the landlord's control (such as an interruption of service by a public utility or by some third party) and one in which it is caused by the landlord (such as failure to maintain the elevators). As to the former, it may be possible to negotiate a rent abatement if the interruption continues for in excess of a specified number of days. As to the latter, the landlord is in default and the tenant has its remedies in that it can sue for damages, right? Maybe not. Watch for language here that seeks to limit the tenant's remedies to the rent abatement.

Covenants in Retail Leases
Here is where the parties go really wild on covenants.

Let's start with the landlord's covenants. This is the flip side of the common area expenses or operating expenses that we were so worried about above. The tenant really wants the landlord to provide the services for which it seeks to charge. In office buildings, with the exception of medical buildings and similar high volume offices, most of the users are employees of the tenants. While that may be a fairly substantial number of persons, it does not compare with the customer traffic at a mall or shopping center. Not only can the center not succeed without that traffic, it cannot succeed if the center is not well maintained and well managed. Good maintenance and management (including security) is critical for the landlord that wants a fully leased center with tenants who can pay their rent and also wants to collect percentage rent on its percentage rent leases. Even though the landlord and the tenant have a commonality of interest in the services, the tenant will still feel more comfortable if the landlord's obligations are spelled out in the lease.

Many tenants also seek exclusives, which I discussed on page 18. Of course, granting an exclusive to a tenant requires that the landlord keep good records so it does not inadvertently default by leasing in violation of the exclusive. The landlord may also have to insert in all its leases a covenant by tenants not to violate those exclusives that, of course, will have to be disclosed to them.

When we look at the tenants' covenants, we find a very extensive list. First, we may find a restriction on a tenant opening another store within a specified radius. This will apply not only in shopping centers but also to the free-standing store, because the purpose is usually to protect the generation of sales for percentage rent. Trading areas were alluded to on page 18. The size of the radius will, no doubt, depend on where the store is located. If the store is in a suburban area, the trading area might be five miles because customers usually drive to those centers, and it is very easy to drive from one area to another. In congested areas, however, the trading area is usually much smaller since, in that situation, the customer must take public transportation or park the car in a parking lot or at a parking meter and it is not convenient to travel five miles to another store location. In that situation, a store five miles away is not strong competition, but a store three blocks away is. The shopping center landlord might want a radius restriction even in leases where there is no percentage rent but it is counting on that tenant, as a destination tenant, to generate traffic in the center and another store nearby might divert that traffic.

Perhaps the most important tenant covenant, however, is what is called the "operational covenant." It is an agreement by the tenant to operate its business in the entire store (except for minor areas for office or storage use) on all days (or on specified days), during specified hours, during the entire term. The landlord wants this principally to ensure that the tenant is open so it can have sales on which to pay percentage rent, but landlords in shopping centers may want it even in situations where there is no percentage rent, because a dark store in a shopping center is a terrible negative for the center. That provision is often the source of intense negotiation.

Landlords are also concerned about where the tenant's employees park. If the employees park close to the sales area or, in the case of a small center, in front of the store, that makes access by customers more difficult. So the lease may require that the employees park in a designated employee parking area and that the vehicles of employees be identified. If the center's parking area is small, the lease may require that the employees park off site.

Landlords in upscale malls are also concerned about the quality of merchandise being sold and will prohibit "going out of business" sales or other sales not in keeping with the quality of the mall. Such leases may also limit sales outside of the premises themselves, except for specified promotions.

In shopping malls, it is not unusual for landlord to require tenants to participate, at their expense, in promotions or to join a merchants' association.

If the tenant is selling food, there will be special requirements regarding trash storage and removal, as well as extermination. The provisions are even more stringent for restaurant operations to prevent venting and sewage disposal problems.

Here is some sample language used by landlords for restaurant leases:

If at any time, the Premises are used for general restaurant purposes, the following provisions shall apply:

(a) Exhaust Systems; Cleaning and Degreasing: Tenant shall, at its cost, prior to opening in the Premises for business and at all times thereafter during the Term, provide the necessary exhaust fans and scrubber systems, ductwork and venting to ensure that all smoke, odors, vapors, and steam are exhausted from the Premises. Tenant's exhaust or venting systems shall include fire prevention and/or extinguishment facilities or systems as may be reasonably required from time to time in view of Tenant's methods and volume of cooking and other food and beverage preparation. This shall be in addition to any sprinkler or other fire protection facilities installed in the Premises. Tenant shall be sure that such systems shall be installed so as to prevent the discharge of noxious smoke, odors, vapors, and steam into the ambient air. Tenant shall regularly and adequately clean or provide for the cleaning of all exhaust, scrubber, and venting systems serving the Premises. This cleaning shall include degreasing of all hoods, filters, fans, vents, pipes, flues, grease traps, and other areas of such systems subject to grease buildup. Tenant shall provide to Landlord, upon demand, reasonable proof that Tenant is doing such cleaning and degreasing or causing it to be done.

(b) Extermination. Tenant shall, at its cost, at all times during the Term, have and keep in force a pest control contract (in form and with a contractor satisfactory to Landlord) providing for monthly inspection and pest control in such a manner as shall eliminate any pest or vermin within the Premises and prevent the spreading of the pests or vermin to other portions of the Property. The contract shall provide that it will not be cancelable by either party thereto except after 30 days' written notice to Landlord.

(c) Sewers and Catch Basins. Tenant shall, at its cost, prior to opening the Premises for business, and at all times thereafter during the Term, provide the necessary piping, connections, grease traps, catch basins, and other facilities for the removal of all waste liquids from the Premises in compliance with all applicable codes and ordinances of the municipality and other governmental authorities having jurisdiction. Landlord may require that Tenant's waste liquid removal equipment include ejector pumps. Such facilities shall be connected to the sewers and mains provided by Landlord, and shall be constructed so as to prevent the backing up or discharge of any such waste liquids into the Premises or into any part of the Property. Tenant shall not dispose of waste grease, oil, or other materials which tend to cause clogging or blockage of pipes and drains (hereinafter collectively referred to as "grease") by pouring or permitting the same to flow into any drains or pipes. Tenant shall regularly and adequately clean or cause the cleaning of all grease traps, catch basins, and similar facilities serving the Premises. Tenant shall not use any chemicals or other cleaning methods which could damage the drain pipes or other portions of the drainage and/or sewer systems in the Premises or the Property. Tenant shall provide to Landlord, upon demand, reasonable proof that Tenant is regularly doing such cleaning or causing it to be done.

(d) Equipment. All equipment installed or used by Tenant in the Premises shall be properly installed and, where necessary, with adequate electrical wiring in conformity with the recommendations of the manufacturers thereof and with all applicable codes and ordinances. No equipment shall be used by Tenant in the Premises unless and until such equipment and the installation thereof has been inspected and approved by the departments or bureaus of the municipal and other governmental authorities having jurisdiction and unless, until, and only for so long as all necessary permits and authorizations for the use and/or operation thereof have been obtained by Tenant from such authorities at Tenant's sole cost and expense.

(e) Trash Removal. Because of the unique nature of Tenant's business, Tenant agrees that Tenant shall store all trash and other waste in odor and vermin proof containers reasonably approved by Landlord, such containers to be kept in areas not visible to members of the public. Tenant shall, at Tenant's expense, attend to the frequent disposal of such materials. Tenant understands and agrees that trash removal must be done by Tenant at such times and in such manner as Landlord may reasonably direct and subject to such rules and regulations in respect thereto as Landlord may, from time to time, reasonably adopt.

(f) If Tenant shall refuse or fail to perform its obligations under this Section, then Landlord, after the expiration of five days after notice to Tenant, may cause the same to be performed, and Tenant shall pay the cost thereof plus an administrative charge equal to 15% of the cost. Landlord shall not be liable to Tenant for any loss or damage that may accrue to Tenant's stock in trade or business by reason thereof, including any loss of revenues resulting from any required limitation or cessation of Tenant's business while performing Tenant's obligations.

Conclusion

You and I are coming to the end, but don't close the book yet. Some important lessons are yet to come!

You may have noticed the frequent use of the word "usually," and also of the words "generally," "customarily," "typically" and "frequently." I am sorry for the redundancy, but there was a reason for it: it is impossible to say that all leases provide for something because that does not happen. On page ___, I said that all leases provide a base or fixed rent and that all leases provide for the use and occupancy by the tenant. I apologize, but I have to contradict myself—even those are not universally true. A landlord and tenant in a retail lease may agree that the tenant will pay only percentage rent, either temporarily or during the term, either because the landlord is very eager to get that tenant into his center and is willing to take the risk on the rent, or because the landlord expects the sales to be so great that it is willing to take that risk, or because of some reason of which I cannot even conceive. Likewise, a tenant may be willing to lease a facility and not occupy it solely for the purpose of preventing a competitor from leasing it, or a landlord's owner may be willing to sign a non-occupancy "master lease" for vacant space as an alternative to a loan guaranty.

So what does all this mean to the lawyer? It means that every lease has surprises! I have been doing leasing since Lyndon Johnson was the President of the United States. You would think I have seen everything, but every time I review a lease for a tenant, I see something new. Sometimes it is innocuous; sometimes it is really detrimental to my client. And sometimes it is so clever that I consider incorporating it in my landlord forms. Further, in representing landlords, I have been working with and revising my forms for my entire career in real estate. Maybe I should have hit upon the ultimate lease by this time, but I keep making changes all the time. In fact, during 2012, I changed my retail lease form 26 times. Granted that many of the changes were suggested by my client's in-house counsel and many were minor revisions, but some were fairly substantial changes resulting from thinking about the issues, or learning of a problem while negotiating leases with the tenant's lawyer and broker, or even from representing a tenant in another retail situation.

There are important lessons for the lawyer in all this.

First, try to digest the lessons in this book about the various types of premises, the various types of leases, and the various provisions in the various types of leases. After all, that is probably why you have read the book to this point. Keep the book around to use as a reference. And it might help us both if you recommend it to your colleagues so you can talk about the issues discussed. Read other sources about leases to increase your knowledge and understanding. Take courses. Do your continuing legal education.

Second, recommend that the broker for your client read the lease as to which you are both involved. If you have used and read the lease form before, be certain that you are advised of any changes made in the form so that you are up to date. Create a comparison from the form used in prior deals so you don't miss anything, and so you can see the business terms more readily. If you are the tenant's lawyer, be sure to read the entire lease. Don't just skim it; your mind may fill in what your eyes gloss over and you might miss some real zingers. Reading a long lease can be tedious, I know since it often is for me. Do it anyway. That is the only way you can effectively represent your client. If you have a question, or if you do not understand something, ask a colleague. Have a stable of other experts, such as insurance agents or construction people, even other lawyers, whom you can call with questions.

Third, encourage the broker to stay involved in the lease negotiation. Make certain that the broker knows that you want him to be a part of the team on behalf of the client. If the broker balks, try to encourage your client to make it happen. Try to assure everyone on the same side of the transaction that it is a cooperative effort, not an adversarial one. Always remember that it is the client who must make the decisions, not you or the broker. If you have a disagreement with the broker about an issue, it should be taken to the client for resolution, but try to present it in a way that does not denigrate the broker or make him or her defensive.

In sum, the more you know, the more you can contribute. Contributing will enable you to become the key player in each lease deal and the result will be more success for you in your profession.

Go for it, and good luck to you!

Index